Praise for Boss Mom

"Dana is a powerhouse of a woman. In Boss Mom, she takes you on a journey from terrified as hell to confident. She will dismiss your biggest fears and will show you that you can rock your business and motherhood without having to choose one over the other. **This book is a game-changer for so many women.**"

- Ashley Beaudin, visionary of #fireworkpeople
and The Firework Box

"**Dana's words are so extremely powerful. At one point I was in tears because I seriously feel like a weight had been lifted.** Boss Mom made everything much clearer to me and to know that my love is limitless and I can give love to both my family and my business without feeling guilty is just such a relief. I'm so grateful. This book is going to touch so many mothers!!!"

– Asheley Freehan, Ashley Freehan Photography

"Reading Boss Mom inspired me to continue working towards my dreams of being a mother AND an entrepreneur. Dana's book lays out a clear message of possibility in the pursuit of developing a strong business. She expounds upon how to work hard to make your desires grow as you grow your family and business at the same time. I read this book after the birth of my third child and it revitalized my longing to be a Boss Mom. **I was exhausted, disappointed about my lack of success and ready to quit, but Dana's words were so encouraging to my weary soul.** I walked through her One Bucket Method for making both family and business work and I have grown as a businesswoman. The book was worth the time it took to work through her suggestions!"

- Danielle Roberts, founder of Legacy Creative Company

"This book is exactly what I needed two years ago when I had my first child. I remember being plagued with guilt that I still wanted to work after my son was born, and that sacrificing all my other pursuits in order to be a "good mother" left me feeling less than fulfilled. The lessons in this book provide a total shift and helped me see the room in my life for mothering AND for working. **Weaving together practical advice, ample encouragement, and deep empathy, Boss Mom gives you permission - and courage - to pursue all of your passions as a mother and as an entrepreneur.**"

- Sonja Jobson, Copywriter

"Dana is an encourager who wants all Boss Moms to know that they CAN have a meaningful career as an entrepreneur and be the kind of mother they desire to be. Not only does she give business tips, but she also shares what has worked for her as a mother. In Boss Mom, Dana speaks openly about launching her business while her children were very young (under two) and gives practical, meaningful, and actionable steps that any Boss Mom will benefit from putting into place. **From the mother who is planning her launch to the established veteran, this book is a must read for any women who is in business for themselves.**"

- NJ Rongner, Digital Strategist and
Blogger at A Cookie Before Dinner

B$SS M♥M

THE ULTIMATE GUIDE TO RAISING A BUSINESS & NURTURING YOUR FAMILY LIKE A PRO

DANA MALSTAFF

Disclaimer: This book is not intended as a substitute for the medical advice of physicians. The reader should regularly consult a physician in matters relating to his/her health and particularly with respect to any symptoms that may require diagnosis or medical attention. All of the opinions expressed in this book are that of the author, and are only meant to be just that, an opinion. The Author and Publisher assumes or undertakes NO LIABILITY for any loss or damage suffered as a result of the use, misuse or reliance on the information provided in this book.

The fact that an organization or website is referred to in this work as citation or a potential source of further information does not mean that the Author of Publisher endorses the recommendations that it may make.

Readers should be aware that Internet websites listed in this work may have changed or disappeared between when this work was written and when it is read.

Paperback ISBN: 978-0-9970451-4-7

Book Coach: Azul Terrones, CoachAzul.com

Cover Design: Madeeha Shaikh, DezignManiac, Freelance Designer @ 99designs.com

Interior Design: Maria Platusic, Platusic Design, platusicdesign.com

Editing: Sheryl Roque

Author Photo: C.J. Thomas, cjthomasphotography.com

Dedication

This book is dedicated to my amazing husband Ryan,
and to my darling children, Jacob and Jordan,
whose love and affection inspired every word,
all of it written from my grateful heart.

BOSS MOM CONTENTS

Welcome Boss Mom!

Part 5: Settling In: The First Few Weeks

Part 6: The First Year: Your Baby's and Business' Infancy

Part 7: Toddler Time: Helping Your Baby and Business Grow

Welcome Boss Mom!

Imagine melting away all of the guilt, fear, and anxiety about being able to be both a passionate mom and a passionate entrepreneur, and replacing them with feelings of confidence, excitement and fulfillment.

What about not feeling so overwhelmed by actually trying to simultaneously raise a family AND a business. Sounds magical doesn't it?

And yes, I did just use the word 'raise' when talking about your business, because your business is also your baby in many ways, right?

Raising and nurturing a family and a business SHOULD be important to you, and you don't have to feel guilty about being passionate about both.

Sound impossible? Don't worry, I'll teach you how.

Now, if you have, like me, felt that heart-wrenching guilt of having passionate pursuits other than just being a wonderful mom, then you know what I'm talking about.

The worry that the world might see you as an uncaring and unloving mother for not wanting to spend every waking moment with your child.

Then deciding to take the plunge to be both a mother and an entrepreneur at the same time, only to continually feel like there isn't enough time in the day, and that your children and your business have constant demands and expectations that you fear you may not live up to.

This is where I tell you that you're not alone!

Then I follow it up by telling you that there is a way, a solution, a path to help you raise both a family and a business and feel that passion, confidence, excitement and fulfillment, without that constant feeling of being overwhelmed.

That's why I wrote Boss-Mom. It was created to accomplish 2 things:

First, to help dramatically shift your mindset about how you see yourself and your role as a mother, entrepreneur, wife, daughter, friend and more. An epic shift that will allow you to see how you can be amazing in each of these roles without sacrificing the others.

Second, to guide you through a new way of thinking about how you integrate your family life with your entrepreneurial life. And to give you a plan that you can begin to implement that will make your world feel a little easier.

I truly believe that this is all possible, because I've lived it. You see, I decided to start my own business and get pregnant at the same time. What? Ok I totally did not plan to do both at the same time. AT ALL. But it happened. There I was going from making good money, to making pretty much nothing, and a baby on the way.

Then came the turmoil of associating my value with my income, and then the guilt about discovering that I didn't want to be a full-time stay-at-home mom. I had to come to terms with the fact that I wanted to grow an amazing business and wanted to be an amazing mom, and really wasn't sure how to do either, let alone at the same time.

Fast forward two years, and my family is thriving, I'm expecting again, running my own successful business, and I feel confident and secure that I'm doing what I love in all aspects of my life, in a way that works best for me and my family.

This book is meant to help you experience the same epic shift that changed my life.

Shed the negative emotions. Be an amazing parent with children who know they're loved. Be a fantastic entrepreneur who has set your business up to succeed by aligning all of your life's priorities, and by having an awesome strategy, allowing you to be that person that gets through the tough times quicker, with resilience and grace.

All of these things are possible, and I will make you this promise...

I believe that there's a light inside of you, and when you feel fulfilled, passionate, and happy, that light shines so bright that it shines on your children and your business and lights them up too. Boss-Mom was created to help give you the tools to let that light shine.

And if you are open to the idea that you can be a passionate mom AND a passionate entrepreneur, then I will help guide you there.

Don't wait another minute. Let's start that journey together right now!

Acknowledgments

There would be no Boss Mom book without each and every person I mention here. Everyone contributed, even if they didn't know it at the time, and I am forever grateful.

From the beginning of everything there was Mom. She was my first hug, my first smile, and I owe my open heart to her. Every day she teaches me how to be an adult without giving up my childlike wonder. She is an inspiration and I treasure her always.

To my step-father, Ilow, who has always seen my potential and not only pushed me to be more, but walked beside me to help me get there. I, without a doubt, owe my mind to him. Every time I joke that 'I must have inherited that from Ilow', it's a testament to just how much he has positively influenced my life.

To my dad, who showed me how important it is in life to roll up your sleeves and get your hands dirty. Every time I watched him build something I learned that we are creatures of creation, and we experience more when we build. Each day that I play with my children I am reminded of how much my father influences how I tackle everyday life. I am so grateful for his love and encouragement.

To my brother, Derek, who I have looked up to my whole life. I treasure our cross country road trips, late night singing, and sci-fi marathons. I won the jackpot as far as brothers are concerned.

To my cousin, Kamee, who is just like a sister, and is the hand on my shoulder that always tells me everything will be ok. I cherish her more each day.

To my absolutely amazing husband, Ryan, who has always supported me. After celebrating our five year anniversary I still look at him and see love, which makes me one lucky lady.

To my fantastically adorable children, Jake and Jo. They don't realize it now, but they are my muse. They light me up in the morning, and melt my heart at night. I am inspired each and every day to be a better me because of them.

To my amazing friends, who have been a part of so many important moments in my life. Each and every one of them has impacted who I am today. To Laura Hannan, Kristen Boniface, Frank Klensch, Daniel Kamas, Katie Howze, Megan Jacob, Kelsey Murphy, Dawn Marrs, and Lisa Anzaldua. And to all of the friends not mentioned here, you are always in my heart.

To Jeff McClain, my mentor and friend, who inspired me to become an entrepreneur and write my story. Thank you!

To the wonderful tribe who helped me create this book. Thanks to Nicole Keating who introduced me to so many amazing people and helped set me on this path. Thanks to Azul Terronez, who has become an amazing friend, and for his guidance on this book, which has changed my life, and helped me find my purpose. Thanks to Sheryl Roque, she saw my vision and helped guide me there through her editing. My book is what it is today because of her. Thanks to Maria Platusic, who made Boss Mom beautiful.

To the amazing Boss Moms who took on the challenge of reading the book in its early stages, and helped create an environment where it can thrive. To Danielle Roberts, Heather Crabtree, Mary Beth Storjohann, Ashley Beaudin, Missy Star, Ashley Freedman, Illiah Manger, Amy Howard, Ashley Staum, Samantha Johnston, Jessica Eley, Sonja Jobson, and Trisha Marie Byrnes.

To NJ Rongner, my amazing digital strategist and podcast bestie, who showed me that we can do amazing things when we work with people we love.

And finally to you and the Boss Mom community. You are more amazing than you could ever imagine and I am blessed beyond belief to have you in my life; thank you for letting me into yours. I can only hope that I get to be someone who helps influence you the way that you have influenced me. With all my heart, I love you!

How to Rock the Book

As you sit back with your cup of coffee, afternoon tea, or a glass of wine, and get ready to read Boss Mom, I want to help set the stage. Let this book be a guide, a friend, and a cheerleader for you. It was written not only to be read, but to be experienced, so when you find the words that speak to you let them sink in.

Boss Mom was written to support you at different stages of life. Even after you've read it once, come back and reference different parts as you go through your journey as mom and entrepreneur. The book, and the Boss Mom community, are there to support you at every stage.

Throughout the book you will find various exercises to help you gain clarity, outline strategies, and maybe get to know yourself a little bit more. To help you rock these exercises, you can go to **www.boss-mom.com/BMBresources** and download all of the activities in this book, and a few extras, all for free.

If you find yourself nodding your head as you read Boss Mom, then you might want to join the Boss Mom community. We would love to have you. Simply go to **www.boss-mom.com/join** to join in, get support and tools to help make your Boss Mom world a little easier, as well as an invite to join is in the Boss Moms Facebook Group.

Ok, let's jump in and get started!

PART 1: THE MINDSET SHIFT
2 Essential Truths

1

Love Has Limitless Capacity

I was recently asked if I'd be taking time off from work when my daughter is born (spoiler alert, I'm expecting my second child). Seems like an easy question, right? I confidently answered Yes AND No. If you would have asked me that same question when I was expecting my son two years ago, I would have quickly said yes, isn't that what you're supposed to do? I mean any other answer at the time implied I was going to be a bad mother.

Well thankfully my mindset has changed, and so has my overall joy in the world.

When I think back on the stress and anxiety of wondering if I should stay at home with my son, I remember being afraid that if I didn't want to stay home with him that meant I was a bad mother, and if I did, that I would be giving up everything else in my life that I loved. Not sure why I saw things so black and white, but there it was… one or the other.

Within 4 weeks after giving birth it was clear to me that

I didn't want to be a stay-at-home mom. Enter a whole bunch of heart wrenching guilt. It was tough. I would long for him to take a nap so that I could spend a little time on my new business. Ok, sprinkle in a little more guilt in there.

There was no question that I loved my son. I was passionate about being a great mother, giving him everything he needed, showing him love, kindness, silliness, and more. **BUT I ALSO HAD THAT SAME PASSION FOR MY BUSINESS, AND IT MADE ME FEEL LIKE I WAS CHEATING MY SON OUT OF SOME PART OF MY HEART THAT WAS SUPPOSED TO BE HIS.**

I couldn't shake the guilt, but I couldn't stop building my business either. It was in my blood, in my heart… it was part of my purpose… part of my nature. For those first few months I continually felt the guilty tug-of-war between making my business one of my priorities, and worrying that if I stopped I would resent my son for taking away something that I loved… even though that was something he had never asked me to do.

I was nervous to let anyone know that I felt this way, but I finally decided to talk to a friend who had also recently had a child. I was floored to hear that she was struggling with the same feelings! Our ambitions weren't exactly the same, but the desire to fill her day with more than just mother/son time was important to her, and she was feeling that same guilt. WOW… I wasn't the only one.

Once again, I have no idea why I thought I would be the only mother who ever felt these pangs of guilt, but somehow

I had allowed myself to feel isolated and alone.

Looking back now, it all seems so silly. I mean, before we have children we live full and wonderful lives, right? Life doesn't start for us the moment our kids are born, so why would we assume that life after their birth should only include them? There's so much more to us than just being a parent, and as it turns out, that's what gives us the ability to be a great parent. But realizing I had a full life before I had kids wasn't what helped me create the epic mindset shift needed to squash the guilt; it was something else entirely.

I HAD TO EMBRACE ONE SIMPLE AND ABSOLUTE TRUTH... THAT OUR HEARTS HAVE LIMITLESS CAPACITY.

Yep, that's right. We don't wake up each morning with exactly 16 grams of love available to us. Love isn't like time where if you don't use it wisely you can never get it back. Love is ever flowing. Love has no measurable size; it continues to expand out like the infinite universe moving ever outward towards the unknown. When you accept this, internalize it, breath it in, and allow it to settle in your soul, then you'll begin to see how this idea can create such an epic mind-shift.

When this new mindset begins to take hold, then all of a sudden we stop worrying that our love for our business somehow detracts from our love for our family. And yes, I just used the word love for your business. After all, you started your business because you wanted to create something and bring it to life. Your business, in many ways, is your baby too; a baby that sometimes cries and wakes you up in the middle of the night, but one that you absolutely love all the same.

I really want to drive this idea home because I believe that it's one of the main pillars that holds us up and keeps us steady. It's what gives us the strength, motivation and confidence to accomplish everything important and valuable in our lives.

Now you might be thinking, if I love everything then doesn't it dilute the meaning of love?

Great question, and the answer is no. You can't dilute love. The more love you put out into the world the better. You go ahead and love your babies, your business, your family and friends. Heck, fall in love with that ice cream, love that blouse, love that song, love that person, thing, or place. You might love certain things more than others, but never stop loving all that you can. The more you decide to love, the more you'll find there's more love available for you to give.

Think of the Grinch in the children's story 'The Grinch Stole Christmas'. He could barely hold that huge load of stolen gifts, but when he understood love, his heart grew 10 times its size and all of the strength he needed was available to him. I love that point in the cartoon when they show his heart grow until it bursts from its little frame, and his smile goes from creepy to adorable just like that. There's a reason this story is so important for our children to see. This story, and all fairy tales, show our children certain truths of life. Truths that are masked by fun characters and exciting songs, but when we dig deeper we find that they're teaching us how to have love, compassion, empathy, charity, humility, and so much more. Einstein once said, "If you want your children to be intelligent, read them fairy tales. If you want them to be more intelligent, read them more fairy tales." I love that he used the word 'intelligent' because it says to me that we can be exposed to a lot of information, but we become intelligent when we truly understand the really important aspects of life. My step-father always said, "Information is not knowledge". We must decide to take what we see in the world, internalize it and make it our own; that's when books like this and stories like the Grinch can help make profound shifts in how we lead our lives.

Our 'aha!' moments may all come from different triggers, but hopefully the result is the same; that you will know that your heart can continue to grow 10 times, or 50 times its original size, with no end in sight. You'll know that love is a driving force that gives us strength, courage, and happiness. And boy, don't we need all three of those to raise a family and a business.

That same strength is what you're given when you have to wake up to feed your infant, take care of a teething toddler, or soothe your child after a nightmare. It's the strength that gets you through when you have to get up painfully early to get that project done, or prepare for that meeting. It's the strength that helps you overcome the challenges that being a parent and an entrepreneur bring each day. It's love that's giving you that power. You might have heard it referred to as drive, determination, or a million other names, but I believe that behind those concepts, there is love. Love has the power to remove boundaries that you might have unconsciously set for yourself. Drive and determination have limits, but love, love is ever growing.

Have you ever felt that sensation when your child, or someone you love, does something just adorable, and your heart feels like it might expand right out of your chest? Well, that's love growing. If you allow that same love for your business, then any limitations you thought existed suddenly disappear. As an added bonus, you stop thinking that being passionate about your business might mean that you won't be the amazing parent that you want to be. **YOU BEGIN TO REALIZE THAT BY GROWING A BUSINESS BASED ON SOMETHING THAT BRINGS YOU JOY, YOU'RE SHOWING YOUR CHILDREN THAT WORK DOESN'T HAVE TO BE SEEN AS A NEGATIVE WORD.** You realize that by being passionate about building something you love, your children will see how following your passion, and working hard to create something wonderful, helps bring more joy into your life.

This is the epic mind-shift that I experienced after having my son that changed the way I've built and grown my business, how I raise my children, and how I ultimately enjoy my life and all of the challenges and experiences that come my way. This epic shift has helped me shed the guilt that makes life seem so much harder than it needs to be.

So take a minute, take a deep breath, and repeat over

and over again that love is limitless. Tell yourself each day, that your heart has more than enough room to love your family and your business, and extra to spare for all of the other things you love in your life. The more you say it, the more you will know it to be true, and the more it will help your business and your family thrive.

Right about now you're probably excited about this idea, and wondering what it means in terms of the right amount of time to spend building your business vs being with your family.

That brings us into the 2nd essential truth.

2

The One-Bucket Method

There's no such thing as balance. I know as moms and entrepreneurs we are always talking about trying to find a good balance, I find myself saying it too. But chasing 'balance' is like chasing happiness. When you think about it as an end point you'll never get there.

When you visualize the idea of balance, a picture comes to mind of carefully measuring sand, constantly adding a little more sand to each side to ensure that everything is even at all times. That sounds exhausting. Besides, sometimes different parts of your life need more attention than others, and you don't want to fall into the trap of continually feeling guilty about that.

Here's the good news. There is an alternate solution to the dilemma… Conscious Integration.

What do I mean by conscious integration? It means that we no longer see work and family as two separate things. I always thought it was funny that we called it a work/life balance, as if work was somehow not part of our life. Every moment we experience is part of our life, so why would you want to separate it out into different buckets? Then all you have is a bunch of small buckets of different aspects of your life you have to manage, and that also sounds exhausting. Instead, let's think of life as one big, wonderful bucket, or as my son would say, 'one big but-it'. It might seem less organized, but by not thinking of life as so many separate aspects of yourself, you're able to prioritize quicker and with more flexibility.

Have you ever heard the story about the professor with the jar of rocks? It's a story about setting the right priorities. The Professor puts large rocks in a jar and asks if the jar is full. The class says, 'Yes'. He then pours a bunch of small pebbles in the jar. The pebbles fill up the spaces in between the rocks. He asks again if the jar is full and the class says, 'Yes'. Finally, he pours sand into the jar. He explains to the class that if you deal with your most important priorities first, then you can see how much room is left for the less important things in your life, and often times there's more room than you thought. If you've ever seen this example on YouTube or in a training class, then they usually start by filling the jar with sand to show you that if you spend all your time on the small stuff, then there will never be enough room for everything else.

What they don't talk about in this popular example is that we tend to have a business bucket and a personal bucket. Odds are, both of those buckets are full, if not overflowing, and unless they've successfully brought cloning to the market when you're reading this, you're going to have a tough time tackling everything in both buckets. The issue with thinking of your business and family as separate buckets is that there is only one of you, and if you're setting your business priorities without thinking about your family priorities, and vice versa, then you're going to find yourself with two full buckets, a lot of stress, and not nearly enough time.

The key is to only have one bucket. Let's call it your life bucket. Now when it comes time to think about your biggest, and most important priorities, you have to think of every aspect of your life together. If your bucket only has room for 4 large rocks, then you're able to start getting really clear on what aspects of your family life are non-negotiable and what aspects of your business are essential to your success. By using this approach to how you set your life goals, priorities, and time commitments, you're able to start getting really clear on what's important and what you can actually fit into your life at any given time.

Taking the one-bucket approach is a powerful way to help strip away some of that stress and get you clear on what you really want to be doing with your days. But the real power comes when we're able to use our understanding of raising a business to help us be better parents, and vice versa. When we begin to truly think in terms of conscious integration we're able to see the endless overlapping in how we raise a business and raise a family.

Now, I wish I could tell you that by embracing these two essential truths you'll never get stressed out, or that challenges won't come your way, but that would be unrealistic. However, if you allow these ideas to truly shift your mindset about how you raise your family and your business, then the tools provided in these pages can lay a foundation for your life that make all of those challenges a whole lot easier.

So let's have a little fun and start at the beginning. You know, that time in your life when you started to ask yourself those 2 questions: do I want children, and do I want to start my own business.

You may not have asked them at the same time, and you may have already known the answer to both, but at some point you made the decision that you wanted to try.

And that is where our story begins.

PART 2: READY OR NOT?
How to Decide if Now is the Right Time

3

Don't Fight Your Boss Mom Nature

Do you remember when you were a child, sitting in your room imagining your future? Do you remember what you wanted to be when you grew up? A ballerina, a doctor, an astronaut, (insert your childhood dream here). The future seemed simple, we knew what we liked and what we wanted to be. We didn't question it. We didn't worry about it. We simply decided and that was that. And if we decided to change our minds, that's what we did, without hesitation.

Life was so much simpler back then. When did we start to question who we are, what we want, and our ability to get it? When did figuring out what we're passionate about, and what makes us happy become so difficult? And when did we stop thinking we could have what we want, or that there were more important things than following our passions?

I often joke that I miss the times when my toughest decision was whether to play on the swings or the slide. We knew what we wanted, and we would repeat it over and over and over again until someone heard us. I mean, literally repeat it over and over again; my son does it all the time.

But alas, as time goes on, our lives get more complex; there is more to remember, more options to weigh, and more responsibility to shoulder. Our purpose and passions often seem to fade into the background, and we begin to deny our very nature. You know, the things in our lives that get us so jazzed you would think we had our own theme song playing every time we did them. The things that drive us and wake us up in the middle of the night because we're so eager to get started. Unfortunately, that very nature is often replaced with the nagging feeling that paying bills, saving for retirement, and cleaning the house are the only really important things in our lives.

So how did this tragic shift happen?

Well, when we're young we see the world with such wonder because it is all so new. We're so carefree because we're often guided by our family and teachers, and most of the logistical aspects of our lives are managed for us. As we get older we begin to create a rolodex of experiences. The sound of leaves in the wind is no longer so fascinating. We've cataloged it and stored it away under 'Sound of Leaves' in our mind. We somehow believe that since we've had that experience before we can simply recall it in its entirety sometime in the future. By the time we're adults, most of us start to believe that it's time to 'grow up' and worry about those more important things that 'have' to get done. We don't have time to listen to the leaves in the trees and really enjoy that moment because we are just too busy.

The fact is, we know this isn't true. We know that enjoying the little things and having new experiences ARE the important things. We know it, but we still find ourselves missing out on what we really want in life because there just isn't enough time to take care of life's logistics AND do what makes us happy.

But there's a loophole.

When you live your life in alignment with you authentic self, then managing the logistics, and doing what you love can coincide. **YOU KNOW YOUR AUTHENTIC SELF; IT'S THE 'YOU' THAT ACCEPTS WHO YOU ARE BY NATURE, AND USES THAT TO YOUR ADVANTAGE.**

So I say stop making life harder for yourself. Find out what truly drives you and make sure it's part of your everyday life. And if you find that you're passionate about more than one thing, which I bet you are, then give yourself permission to enjoy all of your passions. I have a sneaky feeling that if you're reading this book, then you already know you want to be a mother AND an entrepreneur and might already be both. Good for you! Now stop feeling guilty about it, stop fighting your Boss Mom nature, and let yourself be passionate and amazing at both.

Now, I'm not saying that the idea of being a parent or an entrepreneur isn't a bit scary and challenging at times.

THE SIMPLE TRUTH IS THAT EVERYTHING IN LIFE HAS ITS CHALLENGES; IT ALL JUST DEPENDS ON WHAT YOU'RE WILLING TO FIGHT FOR. And when we stop trying to fight who we are, and stop trying to be who we think we should be, all of a sudden managing those challenges gets easier. Right now it's all about putting down the gloves and inviting your 'true nature' over for tea.

So why is it so important for you to embrace your true nature? Well, my step-dad recently reminded me that success has a lot to do with removing obstacles. It's so simple, but we often don't realize how many obstacles we unconsciously create for ourselves; fighting our nature is one of them. And when it comes to starting a family, or a business, we can be our own worst enemy.

WHEN WE FIGHT OUR NATURE, WE KEEP OURSELVES FROM DOING THINGS THAT HAVE THE ABILITY TO TRULY MAKE US HAPPY. And we all want to be happy, right? And just to be clear, the happiness I'm referring to is not some continual euphoric state of bliss. The happiness I speak of is a general sense of fulfillment; it's a state of mind that helps us see our experiences in a more positive light, and allows us to enjoy more of each day, even when challenges get thrown our way. That kind of happiness can only come when we take the time to recognize our true nature and then give it a big hug.

So stop fighting it. Accept the fact that you're a Boss Mom at heart. I know it, you know it and now you can move forward and begin to raise and nurture both aspects of your life.

4

Assessing Your Time, Finances, and Priorities

There's a lot to weigh when we think about starting a family and a business. We want to be prepared, but it's hard to be ready for the unknown. Whether you're starting a business or starting a family, it's hard to know what the end result will be, and that can be scary. Will you be able to get pregnant? Will you be a good parent? Will people want to work with you? Will you be able to make enough money? And most of all…. how will you find time to fit it all in?

Even after you've started a family and a business, there are still so many unknowns. Each time you get the hang of things, it seems like something changes on you, but that doesn't mean that there aren't ways to fight that fear. In fact, there are plenty of ways to look that fear of the unknown straight in the eye and tell it that you're in charge now.

The key is to be able to assess your time, finances, and priorities so that you can quickly adjust when the unknown rears its ugly head. You know, move like a Cadillac, Sting like a Beamer... ok maybe I've seen the Disney® movie 'Cars' one too many times.

Now when you want to grow a business AND a family at the same time it starts to get tricky. You care about both, so how do you know what sacrifices to make so you can fit it all in? Even the most productive people in the world have to make choices on what to do and what not to do. That's where some good conscious integration comes into play. The trick is to have a true life strategy where you build your business around your family and your family around your business.

SETTING YOUR GOALS

This is the first thing I want you to do: Create a list of your 1, 3, and 5 year goals for your business. If you don't have a business, then part of your goal should be to start one.

I'll give you a few minutes to get started. (enter elevator music here)

Now I want you to do the same thing for your family. And if you don't have one yet, that's ok, part of your goals will be to start that family.

Now take a look and see how much overlap you have on both lists. When I first did this exercise I noticed that my financial goals and vacation goals were similar on both sides. I noticed that my business goal list was very tactical, while my family goals were more emotionally driven. It helped me realize that while I loved what I did, I was looking at my business as a set of tasks that continually needed to get done and my family as a place that was full of love, but not a lot of order. When I threw out the two lists and created one 'life goal' list something magical happened: I started to look at everything in my life as interconnected. I didn't realize it at the time, but I was starting to use the One-Bucket Method.

Creating these lists and then merging them is such an important exercise because it helps get rid of some of that fear. It's true, we allow ourselves to create checklist after checklist of everything that needs to get done in our lives. We constantly tell people we are 'so busy', but ultimately, we're the ones that decide what will fill our day. When we create a life-list with intention, one that integrates every aspect of our life, then we can see our true overarching goals, and then gauge all of our actions off of those goals. If you start to do something that's contrary to your life goals, then you can be more confident that you'll catch it quicker, and be able to change direction.

THE TIME DILEMMA

When I polled the Boss Mom community about their biggest challenges, they almost unanimously said… time. I hear over, and over again, "My days are always so full, how on earth I am going to fit a baby or a business into an already full bucket?" It turns out there's this funny paradox about time… when you fill your life with things that matter to you, then you stop worrying so much about not being able to fit everything into each day.

I remember a time when my husband came home and I asked him if he had anything he had to do for work that evening, and he replied that he always had something more to do. It struck me that this feeling that we're never done is so common, and I thought about how stressful that feels to always have more to do. But then later it dawned on me that our feelings of accomplishment and calm don't necessarily come from getting everything done; it comes from celebrating doing the things that matter most. When we tie our daily tasks to a larger goal, it's easier to see how far we've come, and then we stop telling ourselves that there isn't enough time, and start enjoying the time we have.

So what are those larger goals? Well, go back to that one life list you made earlier and see what you wrote. Check in with yourself each morning and look at what you want to accomplish. Whether it's to hang out with your kids, finish a proposal, or work on your website, think about how each task is helping you reach your goals. Everything we do has the ability to help us achieve something, and when we begin to look at everything in our lives as something that helps us reach a larger goal, then you stop thinking of it as wasted time or time taken away from other parts of your life.

Now the tricky part comes when you start to look at your day-to-day tasks and you realize that most of them help you move towards your life goals, but you can't seem to fit them all into one day. Then what do you do?

Well, each day we're faced with tasks and priorities and each day we need to choose what we'll do. If you're already a mother, then you've felt the guilt that your business has come first on some days. I'm here to tell you that it WILL come first on some days, and your family will come first on others. Don't feel guilty about it. **AS LONG AS YOU MAKE CONSCIOUS DECISIONS EACH DAY THAT REFLECT YOUR LIFE GOALS, THEN GUILT WILL HAVE NO PLACE IN YOUR SCHEDULE.**

Think of it this way. You're watching your child at the playground, and as they play you're keeping an eye on where they're running and who they are playing with, all the while assessing what's going on so that if something should go wrong, you can swoop in and make sure everything is ok. But if something should go wrong, like a fall, or a scraped knee, of course you would wish it hadn't have happened, but you also know that you were watching, you were present, and well, sometimes things happen.

When we pay attention to everything around us, there's less room for guilt, because we're clear on what's happening and we're able to assess and take action as needed. **I'M NOT SAYING THAT EVERYTHING WILL ALWAYS BE AMAZING BECAUSE YOU LIVE A MORE CONSCIOUS LIFE, BUT YOU WILL BE MORE CONFIDENT IN YOUR DECISIONS, AND I'M A FIRM BELIEVER THAT CONFIDENCE IS A GUILT-KILLER.**

So whether you've started a family or not, know that time might be scarce, but you'll find a way to fit the important things into each day. And when it feels overwhelming, you can look to the Boss Mom community and know that we're here with suggestions and support to help you get back your calm.

ASSESSING YOUR BUSINESS

When it comes to assessing your finances there's a lot to factor in. I wish I could tell you that if you just love enough, and try hard enough, that success and wealth will be yours, but that isn't always how things work out. With that said, a little strategy goes a long way when it comes to knowing what you can afford when planning for a family or a business.

Let's start with your business first. Before you take the plunge, assess if you really know what you want to do. Do you already have experience, or will you be moving into a completely new field? Will you need to spend money to get certifications, or are you set to go with your existing experience? How will you make money? What will your clients look like? Do you have a partner who will help you to get things started, or do you have to generate a certain income by a certain date? These questions will help you gauge how quickly you will need get up and running, and how much it will take.

The two best pieces of advice I ever received about starting a business was, first, to know your ideal client like they were your best friend. The more you know about who your ideal client is and what drives them, the easier it will be to win their hearts. And second, that you have to identify the urgency in their need. You need to make sure that your ideal client sees what you sell as something they need, and need right now. Later, I would realize that this often was simply a matter of how I phrased my copy.

Now after several years in business, I can confidently say that the following five things are important elements to invest in your business right off the bat. If you do these things right from the start, you'll save a lot of money in the long run and become profitable much quicker.

1   **A BRAND STRATEGY**: Take the time to really figure out how you want to be seen. If you can start your business with a simple and cohesive way that you talk about you and what you do you'll be way ahead of the curve. If you need help with that, download a free workbook on how to create a brand strategy, you should

2   **KNOW WHO WILL LOVE YOU**: This is my way of saying know your ideal client. And don't just figure out the simple demographics of age, gender and income, find out what movies they watch, books they read, podcasts they listen to and what makes them smile. The more you know the better. This will help you learn how to talk their language in a way that pulls them in. The goal isn't just to get people who buy your services, it's to create a tribe that wants to shout your name in the rain and tell the world how you've changed their life.

3   **DON'T TRY TO SERVE EVERYONE**: This one is the hardest. When we start our business we get this knot in our stomach at the prospect of turning away business by not appealing to everyone. You should fight every urge to be all things to everyone. From my own personal experience,

you'll only end up doing work you don't love, making less money, and having clients that don't really understand your true value and worth. Which leads us to #4...

4 **FIND WHAT COMES EASILY TO YOU, AND SEEMS DIFFICULT TO OTHERS**: If you've ever heard someone tell you, 'wow you made that look so easy,' then you know you're on to something. If you can capitalize on what comes easy to you, then making money doing that one thing will be easy too.

5 **GIVE YOURSELF PERMISSION TO CHANGE YOUR MIND**: No matter how sure you are of things when you get started, you will change your mind in one way or another. If you're anything like me, you might just change your business altogether at some point. Listen to your gut, let it guide you towards a business and life that truly works for you, both mentally, spiritually, and financially.

When it comes down to it, if you want to grow your business you have to be prepared to invest back into your business. You might have heard people say that they built their business with a few hundred dollars, but my guess is that that's not the norm. If you're going to build something you love, then take the time to understand which resources make the most sense for your business, and then include them in your budget. If you want a little support to help you select the right resources for you, then head over to www.boss-mom.com/BMBresources.

The site also provides a business calculator to help you see how much it would cost to get your business up and running, and then the cost to take it to the next level.

ASSESSING YOUR FAMILY

How do you know when you're ready? That's the big question. I know women who leapt off of that cliff without hesitation, and then I know how I felt, which was completely petrified. No matter what end of the fear spectrum you're at, here are a few things to think about that can help you know if you're ready to take the plunge and start trying to make a family.

⟨ **IF YOU WANT TO WORK FULL TIME AFTER YOU HAVE KIDS, CAN YOU AFFORD TO PAY FOR DAYCARE?** This might not seem like a question you need to ask yourself right out of the gate, but if you don't know the answer, you might run into issues once the time comes. If you aren't a 100% sure you want to stay at home with the kids and try to run your business during nap time and in the evenings, then knowing how much you can afford for daycare and being clear on that up front can save you from possible frustration later. We knew we could afford my son's daycare, but once my daughter came along we both agreed that my income would need to be able to cover her daycare, or there would be issues. It's something I actually have built into my monthly budget so I know that I can always contribute at least that much each month. The point is that you don't want to feel resentment for trying to raise a family and a business at the same time, or feel like you can't get the support you need. No matter what you decide, it's always important to have that conversation early.

2   **WORRIED ABOUT GIVING UP LATE DINNERS OUT, AND LAZY WEEKENDS?** Yes, it's true that these will become scarcer, and your idea of a good night's sleep will be oh so very different from what it is now. In fact, your life will never be the same again. But I don't say that to scare you, I say it with the knowledge that ultimately those sacrifices are nothing compared to the love and joy you'll feel for your family. A friend recently told me that each day there's about 20% pain, 20% good, and 60% bliss. It totally resonated with me because on any given day I go through a range of emotions from frustration when my son doesn't want to put his shoes on to go to school, to moments of such joy when he runs over to give my husband a kiss, or asks me to sit next to him and play with his train. Each day I have challenges, but those challenges are surpassed by the love of a child and the knowledge that I brought a chubby little life into the world. So know this, it will be hard at times, maybe right from the moment you get pregnant, but everything worth having in life comes with its own challenges. Having a child has been such a blessing in my life, and I

believe it will be in yours too.

3   **ARE YOU NERVOUS YOU WON'T BE ABLE TO GET PREGNANT?** This is always a possibility, for sure, but I believe if you approach it with a little bit of fun you can take a lot of stress out of the whole situation. And besides, if you want children, won't you kick yourself for not trying?

4   **WILL YOU HAVE ENOUGH TIME TO RUN YOUR BUSINESS AND HAVE CHILDREN?** If you use the One-Bucket Method then I believe it's possible to have both without getting completely overwhelmed. The key is that you want to make sure to take all of your family needs into consideration when you're planning how your business will function once you have kids. Odds are your business will not go on as it always did before the little tykes came along. If you consider the time constraints of when you will be taking care of the kids, like the fact that they get up early so you won't get work done at that time, or they might get sick and sent home, then you'll be able to adjust your business to work around your family's needs.

In the end, I can only give my personal beliefs, and I believe that if you want to start a family, that you should jump in with both feet and try. And I will put my prayers out into the universe every night that everyone who wishes it, is able to know the joy of being a parent in one way or another.

5

Why Superwoman is Overrated

As Boss Moms we've all had that moment when we believed we could do it all, and we have all had that moment when we want to break down and cry because we took on too much. The fact is that you can very rarely do it all, at least not well, but the upside is that the perception that you do it all is just as powerful, and makes you feel just as accomplished.

These are two very important discoveries in my life, because originally the idea that I couldn't do it all was not acceptable to me. I just couldn't handle the idea that I couldn't be all things to everyone all the time. So when I discovered that simply providing the perception that I did it all was good enough for me, I seized the opportunity.

How did I come to these conclusions? Well, years ago I was sitting at a marketing presentation and they were talking about their campaign for the Crockpot. Their specialty was doing focus groups with the product's ideal clients to really understand what drove them to love the product. What they realized was that the allure of the Crockpot wasn't about being able to cook with less effort (that was important, but not what really drove the purchase). What really drove the purchase was the ability to have it look like you had cooked all day, without actually cooking all day. It was this aha moment for me. **I REALIZED THAT I DIDN'T HAVE TO DO EVERYTHING, I ONLY HAD TO FIGURE OUT HOW TO DO WHAT WAS MOST IMPORTANT, AND WORK OUT HOW TO GIVE THE ILLUSION THAT THE REST WAS UNDER CONTROL.**

Now, I'm not saying that you should hide when you're in financial distress, or when you really need support, those are times you should reach out to those closest to you. I am saying, however, that when you truly assess your priorities and passions, then you can clearly see which items are towards the bottom of the list and figure out if you can come up with alternative ways to tackle those tasks.

The easiest way to understand your priorities and passions in your business and life is to create an 'urgent and important' grid. This is something you may have used in business before. It's a great way to plot out what's going on in your life and I think that it can be a powerful tool to look at all of your priorities in business and in life, side by side.

If you aren't familiar with the grid, simply draw two intersecting lines. In the top left square put 'Urgent & Important', in the top right put 'Urgent & Not Important'. In the bottom left put 'Not Urgent & Important, and in the bottom right put 'Not Urgent & Not Important'. You can get a downloadable version of the grid at www.boss-mom.com/ BMBresources. Simply fill in short statements of your daily and weekly tasks that you currently need to do to keep your home running. Now on the same grid plot tasks for your business. Now here's the part that we never seem to include, but I think is pretty important... take a highlighter and highlight in one color the items that you enjoy doing, and highlight in another color the items you don't enjoy. Feel free to have several shades based on how much you enjoy completing that task.

I want you to keep in mind that having the skills to complete the task are different than actually enjoying the act of completing the task. Make sure you're really honest with what you enjoy doing and what you don't.

For instance, cooking dinner every night would be in the urgent and important box, but maybe you don't really enjoy cooking. This would be something that you could work to figure out ways to cut down on your time in the kitchen while still providing for your family. Maybe you start to create more crockpot recipes, or maybe you work out a plan for your partner to help you part of the week. Maybe you cook everything on Sunday and have meals in containers in the freezer for the following week. I personally use a weekly calendar on the fridge to plot out the meals. If I know that I have a lot to get done one day, then I make sure my meal plan for that day is simple or already made. This helps me take some of the stress out of kitchen time.

The important part to remember is that you can't do everything, and that's ok. You don't need to be superwomen to be an amazing mother and an amazing entrepreneur. I mean, let's face it, even superwoman has to set priorities, she can't save everyone in the world all at once, she has to make choices... and so do you. When you set your priorities and do the things that are most important to you then something wonderful happens... you're happier, more productive, and you give off a shine that looks like you have it all together. **THAT IS WHAT A BOSS MOM REALLY DOES. IT DOESN'T MEAN YOU NEVER CRY, OR MESS UP, OR FAIL; IT MEANS THAT YOU HOLD YOURSELF WITH GRACE AND SELF-CONFIDENCE AND THAT SHINES THROUGH TO THE WORLD AND POSITIVELY AFFECTS YOUR CHILDREN, YOUR BUSINESS, AND EVERYONE AROUND YOU.**

So I say the era of trying to be superwoman is over and so is the era of trying to find a perfect balance in your life. Neither are realistic and both end in more stress, frustration, and burnout. I say we're embarking on a new era, the era of the Boss Mom, where we know that our passion for family, business and community are not only important, but they feed into each other. An era where we begin to use the One Bucket Method to help raise our business and nurture our families in a way that saves us from sacrificing either. An era where we no longer feel guilt, but instead feel a strong sense of confidence in our ability to love all things in our lives and make a positive impact on everything around us. An era where we understand that there will be challenges, and are able to handle those challenges with courage and grace. An era where we embrace the happy moments and use them to fuel the difficult ones. And finally, an era where we support each other as mothers and entrepreneurs without so much judgment, because we're all living a different story, and making our way the best we can. This is the time when all Boss Moms should stand up and say, "I'm a passionate mother, and a passionate entrepreneur, and I know that my love for both is positively impacting my family, my business, and everything else around me."

PART 3: *The Ups and Downs of Conceiving a Baby and a Business*

6

The Hazards of Overthinking

Have you ever woken up in the middle of the night, and before you can fall back to sleep a thought creeps into your mind, and then you lay there for hours just thinking? You think about how you aren't sure where to find the time to get it (whatever IT might be) done. You think about how people will perceive you, how it will affect your family, if it will really make you happy, whether you should be thinking about it this much at all, how angry you are that this silly thing is keeping you from getting sleep, and finally how now you'll be tired tomorrow and won't be able to implement any of the wonderful ideas you just came up with.

Surely, it happens to us all at one point or another, and no matter what that one 'thing' is for you, the fact that you can't shake it from your mind is what keeps you from performing at your best. You know the old Albert Einstein saying, "Insanity is doing the same thing over and over again and expecting different results." When we get into a rut, we get tense, we get frustrated, and we start to lose our ability to focus on what's important, because we're stuck on, what usually turns out to be, the things that we can't control.

YOUR FAMILY

When it comes to starting a family there are things we can control, and things we can't. We can control how much love and happiness we put out into the world, and towards our partner. We can control the amount of nutrients we decide to use to help fuel our body. We can control whether we decide to see the world with optimism or with distrust. We can control whether we will be a person of action, or one of continual contemplation. All of these things deal a lot with how we look and interact with the world. These are the things that we DO have control over. So often we forget that we have a choice, but if we remind ourselves that we have that power, then the things that are not within our control suddenly become a whole lot easier to take in stride.

When it comes to building a family, all of a sudden there is a whole new thought process going on that can quickly lead us into a stressful, frustrating, and negative rut. Will I be able to get pregnant? Will the baby be healthy? What kind of parent will I be, and what effect will kids have on my personal relationships? We wonder, worry, and stress out about so many things before we even get to the pregnant part. The problem is that this kind of stress can actually negatively affect your ability to start a family. There are many studies out there that show the negative impact of stress on ovulation regularity, sperm count, and fertilization. There was one study from Israeli Researchers that found that "women who were entertained by a clown after they received their IVF treatment were more likely to conceive than those who were not."* It sounds silly, but when it comes to getting pregnant, we could all use a little more laughter in our lives.

Remember that list of things we CAN control in our lives? Well, none of those things are on what I like to call 'the worry list'. You can, however, lower that worry and stress by embracing the things you can control. You can wake up every morning and choose to take a deep breath and know that you're putting love and optimism out into the world. You can choose to eat as healthy as possible, and put yourself in a healthy state so that your child has the best chance to thrive. And you can choose to realize that you are doing what you can to create life, and know that the universe will provide in some way.

Of course, if you don't buy the lotto ticket, you can't win the lotto, so there are a few things you have to do in order to create that bundle of joy... but you know what that is, that's the fun part. Make sure you don't take the fun out of it by worrying about the things you can't control.

For those who have tried and tried, with no success, you have my support and prayers. Find a good support system and talk to someone you trust about your best options. The more open we are to dealing with whatever life sends our way, the more we are able to see the good in all that happens in our lives.

YOUR BUSINESS

That 'worry list' I talked about also applies for your business. I think the worry list might even be longer on the business side and it can be a toxic recipe for inaction. We worry about not being seen as an expert. We worry our clients won't see our true value. We wonder if we will be able to deliver everything we promised. And we wonder (in a moment of terror) if the world will think we are a fraud who has no idea what we're really doing. Stop. Re-adjust. These thoughts not only create stress in our lives, but they can also keep us from moving forward in our business.

The funny part is that one rarely knows what they're doing when they start out. No matter how many degrees you have, books you have read, or children you have babysat, when we experience the real thing we are lost in the woods. And that's ok. The reason we hear so much about the power of failure is because everyone fails at some point, in some way, and that experience is the best way to grow.

Just like our family worry list, the business side tends to be made up of the things that don't actually help us move forward. We hold ourselves back from taking action, asking for business, and launching products because we tend to forget one important fact: that even if what we do isn't well received, it was still a success as long as we learned something from the experience.

You might be thinking that when something doesn't go as planned it still hurts, and that may be true, but the sooner you experience that pain and then see how it will help you to reach the success you wanted, the quicker you will move through it the next time.

One of my favorite quotes is from the book 'The Prophet' by Kahlil Gibran. The Prophet is leaving to go back to his homeland and the townspeople ask him questions about different topics. When they ask about love he says, "but if in your fear you would seek only love's peace and loves pleasure, then it is better for you that you cover your nakedness and pass out of love's threshing–floor, into the season-less world where you shall laugh, but not all of your laughter, and weep, but not all of your tears." I look back to this quote every time I get scared to do something because it speaks to the idea that in order to experience true joy, you must be willing to experience pain and loss. It speaks to accepting the risks and continuing to move forward. And most importantly it implies that by embracing our failures we are able to transform them from times of sorrow to times of growth; a growth that can be the catalyst for our greatest successes.

I know that trying to start a business and a family can be scary. I know this because I was scared... I mean really scared. But I also know that you are stronger than you may think. You are capable of such amazing love, grace, and power. You have inside you the ability to create life and change lives. It would be a shame to let a little fear of the unknown keep you from the amazing things that you will create and put into the world.

* You're Kidding! Medical Clown Increases Pregnancy Rates with IVF, by Maia Szalavitz, Time.com, January 31, 2011

7

Don't Tell Your Partner (or Client) You're Ovulating

Have you ever downloaded one of those ovulation apps? You know the one that tells you your 'peak' ovulation days when you're most likely to get pregnant. They can be great for planning if you're actively trying to get pregnant. However, I personally believe that if not used properly, they can actually make it harder to start a family.

Here's the thing… once you've made the decision to start a family, you pretty much want to make it happen right away. You don't decide to go to the movies, and then wait 6 months, right? When you make a decision you want it to start as soon as possible, but that's not how starting a family works. Making the decision is only the first step. Now you have to start trying, which is the fun part… or at least it should be.

But then here's what happens…

That little app tells you it's time, and thoughts begin to rush through your mind. You start to think about how important it is for this to work. You start thinking about how you're both on the same page with starting a family, so he should be in the loop and know that now is an optimal time. You believe that if you have to be stressed out about the whole thing, then he should be too. This is a joint effort after all, right? So you announce that tonight is the night.

Ok, stop there and let's asses why that was a fatal mistake. If you really think about it, why does it matter whether or not he knows that your body is ready to make a baby? It doesn't. In fact, the less he knows, the better. Why, you ask? Well it's simple really. When you tell your partner you're ovulating you immediately change a fun, sexy evening into a graded performance. He goes from thinking about kissing you all over, to thinking about how important his role is in the whole getting pregnant thing, and then he begins to worry, or worse, panic.

Put on something sexy, give him a 'come hither' look, and that's pretty much all you need to do. Don't say anything else, just allow yourselves to enjoy each other and if it's meant to be then the wondrous baby thing will happen, but for now, he doesn't need to know you planned the whole thing. I can't tell you how many women I know have said that telling their partner took all of the fun out of it, and often times made it harder to get pregnant because, hey, if you aren't having fun, then you really aren't in the mood to take your pants off, right?

You might not realize it, but I just described a fatal

mistake that most budding entrepreneurs make as well.

Don't worry, the ovulating idea is just a metaphor when it comes to your business.

When we start our own business we have a tendency to give too much unnecessary information to our prospects and clients. We are possessed by an overwhelming urge to tell them that we don't have much experience or that they're our first client. After all, we want to be honest and authentic. But here's the thing, your potential clients are looking for a certain type of experience; they want to be wowed. You have a choice to create an experience where they have fun, get all of the value of what you have to offer, and feel special too. So don't begin by telling them how important it is for your business that they become a client, or that you are nervous because they are your first client. And whatever you do don't imply in any way that you don't know what you are doing. That will changes their experience, and certainly not for the better. Think for a minute about what experience you'd like your clients to have and then curate that experience. Ultimately, you will be happy you did, and your business will benefit.

8

Unexpected Side Effects
(In Pregnancy and Business)

I might be breaking some kind of mommy code here, but I can think of at least one time during both of my pregnancies where I had a bit of buyer's remorse. You can't help it, there's a lot going on in your body physically, mentally, and hormonally and it can be a bit overwhelming at times. I remember one time right about when I was 4 months pregnant with my son, where I woke up in the middle of the night in a panic attack. My stomach felt so stretched, I was still getting morning sickness, and it dawned on me that I couldn't take this back; I had to see this through no matter what, and that was really scary.

Nobody warned me that I would be an emotional mess at times. Nobody told me that there would be days when I felt like I wasn't ready to shoulder all of this responsibility. And nobody told me that it was ok to feel this way. There were times that I would just sit there crying, wondering what it all meant, and if in some way this was proof that I wouldn't be able to cut it as a mom. I wish every pregnant woman was sent a workbook that told them they would feel like they were crazy every now and then, and that they would be a total hot mess from time to time, and that was totally normal. Boy that would have been helpful.

As I went through my first pregnancy I started to notice there were days when I felt like the whole world had settled on my shoulders. My sense of humor went out the door, and I would read into things without any rhyme or reason. As it was happening one day, I stopped myself for a moment and acknowledged that this was most likely just my hormones talking. When my husband came home that evening I told him, "I'm a hot mess. I want to warn you that I won't think any of your jokes are funny and will probably think you're telling me I'm fat. I feel like I might cry at ALL times, and anything you say can be held against you. I just wanted to tell you now so you know what you're walking into." It became my disclaimer when I was having a bad day, and it did wonders for our relationship. I was honest about being a complete spazz, and my husband didn't feel so confused or afraid to make a joke that I would normally think was funny, and more importantly, he stopped trying to make it better. That simple act of acknowledgement and acceptance made both of my pregnancies so much more tolerable, and it helped me realize something so very important in life. I realized that by taking a step back and honestly acknowledging what was going on in my life, I was able to feel so much more in control. **I WASN'T ALWAYS ABLE TO CHANGE THE FACT THAT I WANTED TO CRY, BUT I WAS ABLE TO ACCEPT THAT IT DIDN'T MEAN I WAS BROKEN OR CRAZY.**

If you've ever had these feelings, worried that you were either broken, or crazy, or worse, then I am here to tell you that you're amazing. I know I may not know you personally yet, but I do know that you've made some decisions in your life that have put you smack dab in the awesome category. First, you care about learning and growth; why else would you be reading this book. Second, if you continued reading past the part where I told you love has limitless capacity, then you have a whole lot of love inside of you. And third, I believe that we all have some awesomeness inside of us just waiting to get out. So you see… you are awesome. You are amazing. You have so much to offer the world through your business and your family. You may not know how you will change the world, but it's in there, just waiting to reveal itself.

Whenever you get the urge to berate yourself and your abilities or value, I urge you to stop for a moment and think about how important your journey is to the world. Those kisses you give your children every morning are going to help them grow up to be confident adults. Those services you provide your clients are going to help them grow their business, or have lasting memories of their wedding day, or get through that litigation. Each day you wake up you offer something to the world, and that something makes you pretty awesome. So own your awesomeness and don't let those unexpected side effects of having kids or starting a business keep you from seeing the bigger picture… you're contributing to changing the world and I think that makes you pretty darn amazing.

PREGNANCY AND HYPER FOCUS

There is another side effect to the whole pregnancy thing: focus. They say you'll get pregnancy brain, and I'm here to tell you that's absolutely true. Even if you're a productive maniac and don't think anything could keep you from getting things done, just the sheer uncomfortableness of being uber pregnant will probably keep you from performing at the top of your game. But that's not the focus I'm talking about. I'm talking about a high-level focus that helps you see what's really important in your family and business. The focus that helps you make the right decisions in your business and the focus that ultimately helps you grow the right business for you.

As I sit here now with a big ole belly, I can already see the transformation this pregnancy is having on my business. One of the great side effects of being pregnant is that you're all sorts of hormonal. Wait, that's a good thing? Yep, you betcha. We were built this way for a reason and I believe that one of those reasons was to become protective over the things that matter most in our lives. When I took a look at my business it started to become clear which parts of my business were worth protecting. I started to see certain tasks and projects that were actually taking away from my ability to reach my goals. I could see little ways certain actions and choices were keeping me up at night and diminishing my energy and resources. I began to get really clear on why it was I was in business in the first place, and my purpose, or 'why', began to show itself more each day. **I STARTED TO GET REALLY PROTECTIVE ABOUT MY 'WHY' AND IT SUDDENLY BECAME EASIER TO SAY NO TO OPPORTUNITIES THAT WEREN'T BRINGING MY 'WHY' TO LIFE.**

So, it turns out that being pregnant has been the best thing for my business and its growth. I simplified my offerings, and started to only work with women who were truly a great fit. I started to ask myself every morning if what I was doing that day would really help me reach my goal, and I stopped doing the things that weren't really helping me grow my business in a way that felt right.

I also knew I was up against a hard deadline. There was no option to just push back my due date because I hadn't finished a project. In fact, I needed to have everything I planned to accomplish done before my due date in case she decided to come early. I knew that once I had our new little girl I would want to hold her and love her, and not have to worry about anything else. Now if that isn't motivation, then I don't know what is.

So as you enter into the 'expecting' phase of your life, I want you to remember two things: You will have bad days, and that's ok. And you should let that protective instinct kick in and direct it towards your business. Think about what you want to protect in your business, and what you might be doing that is putting what's important to you in danger. The unintended side effects of growing a new little life can help be the catalyst that grows your business too.

9

Babies and Businesses Aren't Built in a Day

Give me a 'hell yeah' if you want to live a life pursuing your passions. You know that life... where the word 'work' is a positive word that gets you all jazzed just thinking about what you get to accomplish that day. That life where you feel fulfilled and loved. These are all things that we strive for each day of our lives and the closer we get to our goals the more excited we get. We want to reach our goals so badly that we start to get antsy when things don't go as quickly as we would like. When we start to get antsy, then we begin to rush decisions, and that's when we stop enjoying the ride in anticipation of the end result.

You know the saying that the journey is more important than the destination, well that depends on where you're going. If that destination is getting to meet your brand new baby, or seeing your first product launch then you REALLY want to get to that destination. But that saying is ultimately true, and no matter how amazing the destination may be, we should consciously try to take a breath and not rush the journey.

Each day of our lives we have an opportunity to grow. We decide how valuable and powerful we want to make each experience and how we want to apply what we have learned to our lives. Even those moments of terrible morning sickness, or getting a bad review, have the ability to provide amazing transformation, if we let them. I'm not saying you should learn to enjoy those times, or that you should not hope they pass by quickly, I'm only saying that through the pain and anguish allow yourself to see the light. The light is the fact that you may be feeling nauseous, but realize that your body is working overtime to create everything your baby needs to survive in the world. When you feel like you just want to lay down on the bathroom floor and cry, you can lay there knowing that at that very moment you are helping to build lungs so your child can breathe, and a nervous system so that your child can know the amazing power of touch. I can't take away the fact that you might feel sick at times, but I do believe that we can change how miserable we perceive that that experience to be by how we choose to see the world.

As we get further down the path towards giving birth to either our baby or our business, we have those days where we just want to be at the finish line, but your baby cooks in that little oven for nine months for a reason. If you were to deliver too early then your baby might not be able to breath on their own, or any other number of complications. Our desire to not feel so uncomfortable or to meet our new little one are outweighed by the fact that they need the proper amount of prep time before they're ready to meet the world.

Every time you're working to launch something in your business, think about whether it has had the proper amount of prep time to ensure its success. Just like your baby, if your new product, website, or service comes out too soon then it might not be able to breathe on its own. Then it would need even more support and care than you originally planned.

Unlike your baby, it isn't always so clear when your business is ready to come out and meet the world, but there are some questions you can ask to help you know when it's time.

ARE YOU CRYSTAL CLEAR ON THE PURPOSE OF YOUR BUSINESS, PRODUCT, OR SERVICE? You should know exactly what problem you solve and what transformation you offer the world. This is the heart of what you create. This is what will course blood and life through your business and whatever it is you're creating. Before you can really build something truly valuable, you need to know why you're building it and how it can change the world. When you think about this, make sure you think in benefits instead of just features. If we use the baby analogy then a feature would be that she is born with a full head of hair, and a benefit would be that holding her for the first time will fill you with a joy you will never be able to describe. See the difference? The benefit is the emotional driver. You want to make sure you know what those are because that is what drives you to create, and what drives your ideal client to buy what you create.

2 **DO YOU KNOW EXACTLY WHO WILL LOVE YOU?** Knowing your ideal client is vital to the success of any launch. It is the same as making sure that your baby is going to have a nice, welcoming home to go to when they are born. You want to make sure you know exactly who is going to take your product or services home with them and love and nurture them. You want to know who will want to take pictures of how amazing your product is and share it with the world, just like they would do with their little bundle of joy. You want to know exactly who will not just fall in love with the topic you're covering, but fall in love with you and your way of delivering that service or product to the world. The more you know about your tribe, the more equipped you are to speak their language and connect.

3 **HAVE YOU ASKED AT LEAST 3 PEOPLE YOU RESPECT WHAT THEY THINK?** All too often we create content for our business in a vacuum. We create and we create and don't ask for the support we need to truly be successful. When you are expecting you ask friends about their experience, and share what you are going through so that you can be more prepared when the baby arrives. The

same should go for your business; find friends, family and colleagues that you respect and ask them to take a look at what you have created. You might be nervous that they won't love it, but if that is the case, wouldn't you want to know that from someone you trust before you put it out into the world? If they give you great feedback early, then you have time to make corrections and help ensure a wildly successful launch.

4 **HAVE YOU ENGAGED YOUR TRIBE EARLY ON?** Don't wait until you are done with your creation to tell your tribe. You want to bring everyone on the journey with you. Get their opinions on big decisions and let them help you decide what they would want most. For instance, if you are creating a new logo, take the top three and ask your community which one they like best. The title, subtitle, cover and interior design for this book were all chosen by my community. I narrowed down the options, but they helped me make the final decisions. Now I know I am creating what they want and it helps create engagement and community before I am even done with the book. Don't miss out on the opportunity to share early. You wouldn't go all 9 months without sharing your experiences being pregnant, right? So why wait until after you have finished the creative process to share it with the world. Let your tribe enjoy your journey and help you create amazing content that they need and love.

Being able to answer these questions will help set up a wonderful environment for your product or service to thrive. Now, start thinking about the building part, and I believe the best way to tackle that one is by walking through each trimester, so let's dive in.

10

Getting Your Business Ready for Baby

That moment you realize you're pregnant can be surreal. I remember when I found out I was expecting for the first time I took a picture of the test and sent it to my mom to make sure I wasn't seeing things. Then I took the same test every day for a week. It was hard to believe it had actually happened. I didn't feel different at that time, so the only thing that told me I was pregnant was a little stick with 2 pink lines. It took weeks to really sink in, and that's when the morning sickness started. I think that's the point when I began to realize I needed a plan. I needed to plot out all of the things I wanted to learn before the baby came so that I was as prepared as possible. It turns out preparing for your first child can feel like a full time job.

Just like with a business, learning everything you need to know to get started can feel really overwhelming, but it doesn't have to. There were plenty of books that told me what would happen to my body and my baby each week, but none of them prepared me for the fact that I ultimately still felt like me. You know, that 'go getter' that doesn't like it when people tell me I can't do things. Each woman experiences being pregnant in a different way, but I didn't like people treating me like I was injured and needed help, no matter how good their intentions were. It took me a long time and a second pregnancy to realize that I had some insecurities when it came to my worth. Turns out I had a hard time letting people help me because I somehow felt that it was a negative reflection on my capabilities. When I say it out loud it sounds silly that a huge pregnant woman would take someone offering to carry her groceries as anything other than kindness, but I felt like I needed to still be the old me that could take care of myself.

This mindset drifted over into my business as well. When I found out I was pregnant I had just quit my job 6 weeks prior. I still didn't really know how I would run my business, it was still in its beginning stages. I felt more and more like I needed to prove I could run my own business, in spite of the fact that I felt terrible most of the time and was exhausted those first 3 months. Looking back, I wished I would have let myself just be pregnant. I wish I would have accepted the fact that I did have limitations that I hadn't experienced before. I wish I would have recognized that being pregnant is a job in itself; a really important job. And **I WISH I HAD BUILT IN TIME TO BE PREGNANT ALONGSIDE RUNNING MY BUSINESS, INSTEAD OF PRETENDING IT DIDN'T HAVE A SIGNIFICANT IMPACT ON EVERY ASPECT OF MY LIFE.**

Building anything new can be challenging, and when you are an entrepreneur who is expecting, you should remember that you are doing double duty. This doesn't mean that you can't do amazing things in your businesses while being pregnant, I know you can. It just means that acknowledging that there is a lot of change going on in your life can actually help your business grow, just like your little growing belly.

THAT PESKY FIRST TRIMESTER

Now remember that wonderful side effect where you become crystal clear on what is meaningful and worth protecting in your business? Well, I'll be honest, that might not kick in until after the first trimester. Those first few months can be hard. The experience is different for everyone, but most of the women I know have all experienced some degree of exhaustion, nausea, pain, and the nagging urge to cry. Don't let this discourage you. There is plenty of time in there where you do feel good, and those are the times you need to recognize and seize the opportunity to be productive. And also realize that it's just a short time in a long life, and that the second trimester for many is a time of energy, productivity and fun. So make sure you allow yourself to build rest into your business plan. Sit down on the couch and read a book, watch a show, or take a nap. Don't you dare think of it as slacking off! Your body is hard at work, believe me. Building in that cushion time into your business schedule will help give you the opportunity to rest and rejuvenate, and that resting is what will keep you from getting burnt out or over-stressed in your business.

Once you hit the second trimester things tend to get a bit easier. If you experienced nausea, you probably won't feel as nauseous and you start to get some of your pre-pregnancy energy back. This is a good time for action in your business. You have several months before you will start to get pretty uncomfortable, and you may have started the decorating daydreaming, but you're most likely not in any rush to have everything up and ready. This is a good time to focus on your business and make sure you are preparing for your maternity leave.

DO BOSS MOMS GET MATERNITY LEAVE?

Maternity leave? Do Boss Moms get maternity leave? You bet they do, or at least you should, it just takes a little planning to make it possible. The amount of time you decide to take off is different for each of us, but wouldn't you rather have planned for the time, than to feel like you 'have' to take care of your business when you would rather be cuddling with your new baby? If you find that a week after your baby is born you want to get some work done, then that's great, just set your business up so that's a choice you can make at that time. In other words, don't create a tight schedule for yourself right after the baby arrives. Give yourself time to recover and to get to know your baby, and if you want to get some work done during that time, then you can, but on your terms.

If you are having a hard time imagining how on earth your business could ever run without you, then you're not alone. I felt that way for a long time. They didn't invent the word 'solopreneur' for no reason; we are out there all alone trying to do everything ourselves. That was the mentality I had when I was pregnant with my first child and it ended up causing me a lot of stress and anxiety. There were some pretty unenjoyable times when I wanted to play with my son, but had to spend unwanted time with my business because I thought everything rested on my shoulders.

The first step is to accept that the only way to grow a business is to get support. Help can come in many forms, from hired support, to family and friends. The key is to figure out where you'll need help, what you can hand off to someone else, and what you can get rid of completely.

THINGS YOU CAN GET RID OF ALL TOGETHER

The best first step to prepare for your own personal maternity leave is to take a good hard look at your business, and see if there is anything that really isn't helping your business grow and is taking up a lot of your time. I realized that there were certain projects I had taken on that were time consuming, weren't utilizing my strengths, and weren't paying the money I knew I was worth. Ultimately, this was nobody's fault but my own for taking on work that really wasn't serving my 'why', but when you are starting a business you want to say yes to every opportunity that comes along. As your business grows you begin to see how this strategy doesn't really help you in the long run.

When you start to prepare for time off, you realize that

your time is truly precious, and you don't want to waste a moment that you don't have to. So make a list of everything you do in your business on a day to day basis. List out who you work with and what projects you have. The easiest way to visualize this is by drawing out a t-chart just like we did with the important and urgent exercise. On the vertical axis is the 'like' to 'dislike' scale, and on the horizontal axis is the 'little time' to 'lots of time' scale. You can get a downloadable version at www.boss-mom.com/BMBresources. Take everything you put on your important and urgent chart and plot it out. This simple exercise helps you go a step further and see which tasks are causing the most time drain. Your goal is to get most of what you do each day to go up on the top portion of the chart. This is where all the tasks and clients you like live. If you notice that you have a client that you really like, and they take up a lot of your time, then assess how much revenue they are providing to your business. Just because you enjoy working with someone, doesn't mean that they are a great fit for your business. If they're taking up a lot of your time, but not provided the necessary revenue, then they're taking away from your ability to make income from other places.

Now take a look at everything on the bottom half of your chart. These are all of the clients and tasks you should work to get off of your plate. After all, you started your own business so that you could do what you love, and work with your ideal client. So why are you doing things you don't enjoy or working with people that don't make you feel amazing and valuable?

Some of the things on the bottom half of your chart might be tasks that need to happen to run your business, but that doesn't mean you need to do them all yourself. I recommend looking into a virtual assistant (VA) for a few hours a week to help you do some of those tasks you don't like, especially the ones that are taking up a lot of your time. Often times, the fact that we don't enjoy the task plays into how long it takes us to get it done. You might find that handing certain tasks off to a VA is cost-effective and gets done quicker because it's something they enjoy and do well. If you want to learn more about VA's there is no better book than Chris Ducker's book, Virtual Freedom. It's chock full of amazing tips and exercises to help you get ready, hire, and manage a VA.

If you don't have the funds for a VA, then think about getting an intern. It is actually easier than you might think to get an intern, and if you visit www.boss-mom.com/BMBresources you can download a guide to hiring an intern. The important thing is to stop doing the things you don't enjoy, and the things that are taking up a lot of your time without bringing in the revenue.

Think about it like this, if you could pay someone for less than you would make in that time if you were working with a client, then you are wasting money by doing it yourself. Sometimes we don't want to invest in the support, but by getting these things off your plate, you are free to do other things that can make your more revenue. I know it works because I have done it, and creating a support team has helped me grow my business so much quicker, even when I took maternity leave.

GETTING MORE ORGANIZED

It's really hard to get support and take time off if you aren't organized. A good place to start is to look back at the chart you just made and see what you would like to be able to hand off to someone else. For me I realized I wanted someone to take over managing my blog. I have a colleague who wanted to get her podcast managed, one who wanted her email managed, and another who wanted her discovery calls and on-boarding process managed. Once you know the things you would love to hand off to someone else, you can start to walk through and document the process you currently use to do those tasks. Now I know that the reason most solopreneurs don't document in the first place is because we are too busy running our business, but there are some easy ways to document your process.

The easiest way is to record your screen while you're going through the process. You didn't really take any extra time to document because you had to get the task done anyway; you just happen to record and talk through the steps while you were doing it. Now take that video and create a list of the tasks you walked through, or better yet, have your new VA or intern do it for you. I am personally a big fan of the free project management tool Trello. You can watch a video of how I use Trello to manage most of my processes at www. boss-mom.com/BMBresources. No matter how you record your process, the important part is that you have made it easier for someone else to help you. Now in a crunch anyone would be able to know how you would normally complete the task and that makes getting support a lot easier.

MENTAL SUPPORT

Where else will you need support you ask? Once you have the little one, you will have a lot of hormones pumping through your body. You will have this new little life that needs you pretty much 24 hours a day, and while that can be an amazing feeling, it can also be overwhelming. Plan to get some mental support while you are on maternity leave, and even after you go back to working. Mental support for your business can come in the form of a mastermind group, a coach, or a Facebook group. These are people that you respect and trust, and they will help you make rational decisions about your business during this taxing time.

On the personal side I have found that the best mental support comes from those that have gone through what you are going through now. This might be family or friends, a local support group, or a Facebook group like the Boss Moms group. These women provide support when you run into new mom challenges. Planning for mental support for your business and family is a really important part of getting your business ready for your new mom status; it can be a life saver when you are faced with lots of consecutive sleepless nights.

Now that you have a good idea of things you want to stop doing all together, the things you want to push over to your support team, and where you are going to get your mental support, you should write it all down. You can download the Support Planning Worksheet at www.boss-mom.com/BMBresources to help you get started.

PREPARE FOR A WHOLE NEW WORLD

In most cases, even when you're pregnant, you're still mostly able to run your business as you did before. When that baby comes it is a whole new ball game. Not only are you ridiculously sleep-deprived, but you have a crazy amount of hormones coursing through your body, and a new tiny little life that you just want to stare at for hours. Oh, and they say 'sleep when they sleep', but you just end up waking up to check to make sure they're still breathing, so not a whole lot of rest is going on for at least the first few months, and some parents say it can take years.

I think I can pretty confidently say that once you have a baby your life will never be the same. That also means your business won't be the same either. You might still do the same tasks and offer the same services, but from day one you'll notice differences. These difference vary for each mom, but some of the common changes are: a desire to work a little less so you can hang with your baby, the occasional lack of focus as you remember that cute thing they did that morning, the aching desire to drop everything the second they don't feel well, as well as that guilty feeling when you hope that running nose doesn't turn into a fever because you have a deadline to hit.

The fact is that when you become a mom there is a whole new, and somewhat unpredictable variable in your life and it has a way of affecting you in ways you can't even imagine. If you try to convince yourself that having a baby won't change how you work or how you feel about your work, then you might be putting your success at risk. When you acknowledge that life will be different, then you are able to assess what might change and adjust as needed. Doing this early will save you a lot of stress, frustration, and guilt. That might mean working more with clients who are empathetic to your new status as a mom. It might mean taking on less work, or looking for additional ways to create passive income. It might be adjusting your hours. I don't book anything before 9:30 in the morning so that I can be sure to have some time to hang out and have fun with my kids.

The idea isn't that your business has to be different now that you have kids, it simply means that certain things will change, and the quicker you acknowledge this and assess what really matters to you in your business and family, the easier it will be to ensure your business is set up for your new dual role as a passionate mom and passionate entrepreneur.

11

Embracing Your Emotional Cycle

There's a natural cycle to everything, and within that cycle there will always be ups and downs. We often subscribe to this notion that, when things start to fall through the cracks, feeling overwhelmed is somehow this terrible weakness that must be overcome, but there is no way to live a life completely devoid of those occasional feelings of being overwhelmed. That's right, I said it; being overwhelmed is virtually unavoidable. What we CAN do is see it coming and ride the wave. Acceptance and permission are the keys to helping you recover quicker.

When it comes to creation, there's always a lot going on. Whether you're creating a business or creating life, there are many tiny moving parts, and maintaining continual control can be difficult. I want to give you permission to accept that overwhelming feeling that may come from time to time. Even more important, I want you to give yourself permission to be overwhelmed. Now, why on earth would you want to be overwhelmed? Of course you don't, but that's not the point. The fact is that you WILL feel overwhelmed sometimes, and how you deal with it is what will determine how it ends up affecting your life.

Did you ever see the Disney® movie, The Lion King? Remember the song, The Circle of Life? You might be singing the lyrics right now, but just to help refresh your memory, the chorus goes like this: 'It's the Circle of Life, and it moves us all. Through despair and hope. Through faith and love. Till we find our place. On the path unwinding. In the Circle, the Circle of Life.' You can't help but get caught up in the song as you see all of the animals gathering at the beginning of the movie, but when you really think about the lyrics, they speak to each of our lives. We're all moving forward, whether we like it or not. If you already have children then it's oh so apparent each time you look at your child and realize they're growing and changing right before your eyes. As we move forward we interact and impact each other's lives. We have moments of despair and moments of hope. No matter who you are, these moments are bound to find you at one point or another. When we embrace those moments of despair or of feeling overwhelmed, and realize that they're a natural part of the circle of life, then we can allow ourselves to continue to move with the natural flow of things. It's when we try to fight these overwhelming moments, or punish ourselves for not being in control, that we disrupt the balance and, more often than not, add more stress to our lives.

The fact is that as a parent and entrepreneur, you have an unavoidable complexity in your life. Even when you're doing nothing, you have a lot going on. Add in some extra hormones, a pinch of empathy, and a need to nurture, and you have a recipe for a woman who's going to want to cry, argue, and be completely irrational sometimes. That, my friend, is the natural cycle of things. Own it. Acknowledge it. Embrace it. And don't beat yourself up, because you have a lot going on.

The one thing I would ask is that you take all of that amazing empathy and nurturing nature that I believe is in us all, and warn the ones you love when trying times are coming. We need to get our emotions out in order to restore the balance, but we don't need to leave a path of destruction on our wake. So when you start to feel those emotions creeping up, don't push them down, find a place where you feel safe and supported and let it out.

If you aren't sure where that place might be, here's a good way to figure it out. In the past, how have you felt emotional relief? Is it when you watch a sad movie and experience a good cry? Is it when you are able to talk it out with a close friend? Maybe you meditate or go for a run. Think about the times when you were able to shift your feelings. Write down what that looked like. Each of us deals with these moments in a different way, and there's no wrong way to experience your own emotions. Do what's right for you. Do what works, and if you aren't able to figure out what works, look to your support system to help you figure it out.

Embrace your emotional cycle and see the positive effects it can have on your business, your family, and on you.

PART 4: LABOR AND DELIVERY
Preparation & Anticipation

12

Hypnobirthing Your Baby and Business (Releasing Fear and Changing Your Experience)

I was first introduced to the concept of Hypnobirthing by a friend whose son was due right at the same time as mine. I went home to do a little research and was intrigued by what I found. Like many people, I first thought that it was all about hypnotizing yourself to not feel pain, which seemed pretty unrealistic to me at the time. What I found out was life changing, because Hypnobirthing isn't just about a breathing technique, it's about changing the way one thinks about stress and pain. It raises the notion that we often create much of our own pain by being afraid of pain, which in turn causes stress. Sound crazy? I thought so too at first, but now having used its techniques, I believe it has the power to change how we experience the world. And here's more good news… you don't have to be pregnant to enjoy the benefits! In fact you don't even have to be a woman, everyone can benefit.

HYPNOBIRTHING & LABOR

I remember plenty of situations where a family member or friend who had already had children told me about their terrible, painful and traumatizing labor experience. Come to think of it, I remember being told by a complete stranger in the grocery story about her horrible labor. I was being warned of the terrors that awaited me! Each and every time I could feel my muscles tense up and I began having nightmares. Have you ever seen the movie SpaceBalls? (Yep, I just made a reference to an 80's Mel Brooks movie) If you haven't seen it you should YouTube the scene with the alien in the diner. It's a parody of the scene from the thriller movie Aliens where the baby alien bursts out of one of the crew member's stomach. The SpaceBalls version includes an alien with a top hat and cane singing 'Hello My Baby, Hello My Darlin,' and while it's hilarious in the movie, having dreams that involved a singing alien coming out of my stomach was not cool. When I found out about Hypnobirthing, that all changed.

Hypnobirthing teaches that most of the pain experienced in childbirth is pain created by being scared and stressed out. Our fear and stress causes our muscles to tighten and blood flow to go towards the areas of the body that are needed to flee the situation (you know, fight or flight). And it turns out your reproductive organs aren't one of those parts needed to flee the scene. This means a lot of the pain you feel is self-perpetuated. Without going into the gory details, when your muscles are relaxed, and there's good blood flow, it's easier to have a baby.

Ask yourself whether you believe that women are built to go through childbirth. If you think about it, our bodies do some amazing and creepy things to prepare us for having a baby. One could argue that we weren't built to be a business coach, or a doctor, or a yoga teacher, but we were built to have babies. You won't find any other species deciding that they aren't ready to have kids yet because they want to go travel for a few years, or go get their Masters. So if we were built to have babies, and nature wants us to have more than one, then it wouldn't make much sense to make the labor experience horrifying. Who would want to do that more than once, right?

Once you realize that your body was made specifically for this one particular task, then you begin to trust your body more. Your body will know what to do when the time comes, and the more you let your body guide you, the less it will hurt. It's always important to be mindful of how you feel just in case, so that you can make sure you get the help and support you need should something not go as planned. I can't guarantee that practicing Hypnobirthing will give you a totally pain free labor, but I can promise that if you believe that having a baby is meant to be painful, then you're sure to have a painful experience.

I'll be perfectly honest and tell you that there was some real discomfort when I had my son. There were a few moments where it felt like I had just slammed my knee into the corner of my desk and it took my breath away. But once I took a deep breath and let myself relax, the pain would lessen more and more with each breath. My memory of my labor was one of joy and love, and I was able to have my son in less than 6 hours. This may not be the same experience for everyone, but if you're expecting, I encourage you to check it out, even if you plan to ask for that epidural the second you check in.

HYPNOBIRTHING & BUSINESS

The amazing thing about Hypnobirthing is that it can help you in every aspect of your life. If you take the concept that we create our own pain through our fear, and shift it over to business, then the theory still holds true. You see, it turns out that most parts of your brain aren't required to help you flee. The blood flows mainly to your heart, lungs, legs and back, so getting worried and stressing out about that presentation isn't going to help you. You need the blood flow to the brain so you can impress the crowd; you don't need it rushing to your lungs and legs (even if you are imagining yourself fleeing off the stage). Instead, shift the way you're thinking about the situation.

You have a choice to think about all of the negatives potentially associated with that situation, or to think about all of the positives. You can choose to imagine yourself failing, or you can imagine yourself succeeding. You can choose to see how hard everything is in your life, or you can choose to see all of the ways you are blessed. If you choose to see the negative then you're inviting pain and stress into your life.

When thinking negatively, if you're writing a blog, it will take longer and feel more difficult. If you're talking to a potential client, you'll hear all the reasons why they wouldn't want to become a client, and that negativity will affect your ability to confidently ask for the business. It may affect how the potential client sees you and your personality. If you choose to see the positives and potential, then your ideas will flow easier, things will go quicker, and your confidence will rise.

So what will you choose? Will you decide to see the positives in every situation, and know that you've got this? **IF YOU NEED A LITTLE NUDGE, THEN HERE IT IS: YOU ARE A UNIQUE CREATURE IN THIS WORLD. YOU HAVE SO MUCH WONDERFUL VALUE TO OFFER, AND YOU WERE BUILT TO DO WHAT YOU ARE DOING RIGHT NOW. KNOW THIS, EMBRACE THIS, AND YOU WILL NOT ONLY SUCCEED, YOU WILL THRIVE.**

13

The Birth of Your Aha Moment

I have some wonderful news. My daughter was born on June 30th at 2:17am. However, she came out too fast and didn't have time to do what they call transitioning, so she still had fluid in her lungs. Within a minute of her being born, they took her away from me and rushed her down to the Neonatal Intensive Care Unit (NICU). It was a scary time, but I'm glad to report that within two days she was breathing on her own and back in my arms. It just goes to show that no matter how much planning you do, sometimes life has other plans.

It has been such an interesting journey to start this book while I was pregnant and finish it after my daughter was born. I was originally sad that I had not finished the book on schedule prior to her being born, but I realize now how much more experience I'm able to bring to the table, and now I wouldn't want it any other way. I feel like I say that phrase a lot now that I'm a parent.

Part of my labor experience the second time involved about three days of light contractions and finally a good six hours of walking around the hospital before they would admit me. Lucky they did because I gave birth two hours later. During those six hours I had a lot of time to think and talk with my husband about every topic under the sun. Businesses and babies have a lot more in common than we think. Both take preparation time, building and planning, and then at some point they're ready to come to life. We then work sleeplessly to love, nurture, and help them grow.

During those six labor hours, it dawned on me that part of me, the more vocal part, wanted to have this baby now. The few weeks leading up to labor were filled with me saying things like, "alright already, can't we just have this baby and move on." I know friends who have told me about moments of outbursts like, "get out of me baby", or "I'm done, let's do this". By delivery day we are so ready to start the next phase of life, and that goes for our businesses too. At some point we just want to get that product out there, or launch our website; we want to move forward. And then there's that other part of me, the silent side, that didn't want it to end. I knew what to expect. I felt safe and secure. Sure I was uncomfortable, but I had gotten used to life this way, and now it was all about to change. Even though that change was everything I wanted, part of me secretly hoped it wouldn't happen so fast.

I realized that that silent part of ourselves is often busy at work in our business. We want to launch that product, or get that client and we shout it from the rooftops that we want it to happen now, but something inside of us keeps us right where we are. Some inner self reminds us that it's safe and secure right where we are. Why not wait another week to launch, until everything is just perfect… it'll work out better if you wait. I don't know about you, but me, and just about everyone I have ever worked with has done this to ourselves. **WE YEARN FOR OPPORTUNITY, BUT WE OFTEN TALK OURSELVES OUT OF MAKING IT HAPPEN. WE HAVE SO MUCH TO CREATE AND GIVE TO THE WORLD, BUT WE KEEP IT INSIDE OF OURSELVES BECAUSE WE'RE AFRAID OF WHAT THE FUTURE HOLDS.**

When the moment finally came to meet my daughter, it hit me; the love and comfort that I felt during my pregnancy was just one kind of love. Meeting my daughter and becoming a mother all over again was a completely different love experience, and both experiences were important to making me the kind of mother I wanted and needed to be. I realized that when you create your business, you start yourself on a path to fall in love. All of that preparation, planning, day dreaming, and building brought you closer and closer to what your business would become. The truth is that we put just as much love and effort into building our business as we do building our babies. The more love and joy you pour into both, the more love and joy you have when they finally come into the world.

Now I'll be the first to admit that when I first met both

of my children it wasn't like being hit by a bolt of love. I was exhausted from being up all night, and a little overwhelmed. I remember wondering if that was it; was that all it would feel like to be a mother? But there was so much in store for me, just like there is so much in store for you. Each and every day I love my family more. Each and every day I see new and amazing things about my children, and each and every day I see new and amazing things in my business too.

My 'aha' moment this time around was that love isn't just limitless... sometimes love takes time, and the journey helps create a solid foundation for love to grow.

14

You Can't Put 'Em Back In: When Your Baby and Business Take On a Life of Their Own

People warn you about how hard it can be to be a parent, or an entrepreneur. They warn you about the sleepless nights, the crying, the biting, and the agonizing pain you will feel when you say 'no' to your child and that little bottom lip comes out and starts to quiver. You'll get warned more times than you can count, and it's always followed up with… "being a parent is also the most rewarding thing you will ever do."

There's a reason we get warned. We get warned because it's all true. Being a parent is really, really, really hard sometimes (yes all 3 'reallys' were required). Guess what, being an entrepreneur is also really, really hard. Both your children and your business require your love, compassion, empathy, and sacrifice. Sometimes you won't know what your business or your children want, only that they won't stop crying until you give it to them. They will have days when they don't want to hug or kiss you. There will be nights where they both need constant attention. And your business and kids will look to you to make everything alright; this is the unwritten contract you signed when you decided to become a parent and an entrepreneur.

Being a parent and an entrepreneur can be really hard, but it can also be super rewarding. Both will surprise you in ways you never imagined, and both will live as legacy to the love, compassion, empathy, and sacrifice that you gave to them each day. Being both a mother and entrepreneur just might be one of the biggest challenges you will face in your life, but remember that big challenges are met with big reward, and boy do babies and businesses know how to show the love.

Imagine the first time your baby tells you they love you, or the first time a client tells you that working with you has changed their life. Imagine how you'll feel in those moments and know that it will feel even better than you could imagine. I imagine your cheeks will ache from too much smiling that day. Breathe it in and let it settle in your soul, because those are the moments that will carry you though the tough times. They're the moments that remind you what love feels like.

Of course, there might be moments where you just want to quit. There might be times when you need to just set everything down, even your baby, and walk away for a few minutes. There will most definitely be times when you wonder what the heck you're doing all of this for. Don't kick yourself too much. Remember that life comes in cycles, and you just might be hitting the peak of the storm before it breaks. Don't let these moments discourage you from your overall goals to raising an amazing family and a successful business. There may be tough times, but let those wonderful, amazing moments help keep you going.

15

Second Time Around: Wiser… Or Are You?

W e always hear that experience is the best way to learn, and when it comes to babies and businesses that's without a doubt true. No matter how many books you read, people you talk to or videos you watch, nothing can truly prepare you for what lies ahead. You have to jump in, take what you've learned and fill in the blanks with what you think will work best for you. There's a lot of trial and error when it comes to starting a business and a family, and that's how you get comfortable with your decisions. You try things out, see what works, and go with it. Every child is different, every business is different, and that means each time you have a baby or start a business, there's a whole new set of circumstances that will require more trial and error.

The second time around does offer up a few wonderful benefits. Once you have a baby you know you can do it; you know you can survive. This one idea is more powerful than you can imagine. You've just stamped out the fear of the unknown. Was it hard to do, sure? Is it something you want to go through often? Maybe not. But you know that you made it to the finish line and created something new in this world. You're one awesome lady, and you know it now. And every time you question it, remember all that you have accomplished so far.

Each day you learn a little bit more. Each day you try new things out and see what works. Each day your worry meter goes down just a little bit because you're becoming more comfortable in your new role as a mom. Those things you lost hair over when your baby was first born are now starting to become routine. You know, things like checking on them 10 times to make sure their breathing, spending 2 hours trying to figure how to install the car seat, or stressing over whether that's a hungry or gassy cry. After a while you start to recognize their cries like unique bird calls and walk with confidence and pride to go save the day with just the right solution. Your 'get ready' time goes from 2 hours to 20 minutes as you throw just what you need into a bag, head for the door, and click everyone in with ease. Shoes, bottle, diapers, blankie… check, check, check. You've got this mom thing down.

Those same strides happen in your business too, but instead of 2 hours with the car seat, you're spending 10 hours trying to figure out your website. You scroll through website plugins, and business resource articles just like you poured over websites to build your baby registry. You read recommendations and ratings and try to figure out which email marketing manager to use just like you tried to figure out the right type of diapers to get. You might have even cried a few times when something wouldn't format correctly, or no one was signing up for that workshop you created. Just like with your baby, you get better as time goes on. One day you wake up and a pesky website issue gets resolved in minutes... or better yet, you now have a go-to person for just this kind of thing. And suddenly, your workshops begin selling like hot cakes, because you learned from trial and error where to market and how to speak to your tribe.

This experience gives you 3 invaluable things: confidence, time, and expertise.

You stop questioning whether you can actually run a business or raise a baby; you know you can. You confidently call yourself a mom and an entrepreneur... or a Boss Mom for short. You not only save time by reaching into your vast toolkit of experience and pull out the answer quicker, you also know how to tackle new problems with more grace and ease. People start to ask for your advice on how to run their business. You go from always being a mentee, to also being a mentor.

All of this experience can sometimes give us the false illusion that because we did it once, we can do it again without any issue. Had a baby once? How hard could two be? Already started a business, how hard could a second venture be? They might not be as hard as the first, but don't be fooled, there'll be some new growing pains that will blindside you on some idle Thursday.

Remember those unique cries you learned for your first baby? This second one will have all new cries that baffle you for months, and no amount of knowledge from the first baby will help you. You'll simply have to take the time to get to know this new baby and learn their little unique traits. Remember the way your ideal client reacted to a certain kind of content? This new business doesn't respond the same way, and you have to figure it all out again. Don't be discouraged, you're still going to be quicker, better, and more confident the second time around. The key is to remember there is a new set of variables and that means new uncharted territory. Some things might work like they did before, and some might not. Allow yourself to recognize then your past experience isn't helping and jump back into trial and error mode. Don't let it get you down, know that recognizing when you don't know the answer is a wonderful sign of intelligence.

So are you wiser the second time around? I would like to think so, but then again recognizing we still have a lot to learn is the ultimate sign of wisdom, right?

PART 5: SETTLING IN
The First Few Weeks

16

Always On:
The Joy and Pain of Being Needed 24/7

The joy you feel when you're the only one who can soothe your crying baby is something I will never fully be able to describe. The best I can do is to say that it feels a lot like being bathed all over with fragrant rose petals by little gnomes whispering that you're amazing. Ok maybe I have a strange way of describing things. I imagine that feeling you get when someone else truly needs you feels unique to each of us, but it can also be a double-edged sword.

It would be wonderful to only be needed after you've had a full night's sleep, or eaten a nice yummy meal. Those, unfortunately is rarely the circumstances when you're a parent, or an entrepreneur for that matter. Those moments when we're needed the most are usually when we can barely keep our eyes open, our sciatica is flaring up, and all we've eaten lately is 2 slices of slobbered on apple and our daily vitamin. Love pushes us forward as we hear that heart wrenching cry for 'mommy' from the other room. It's nice to be needed and loved with such fierce sincerity.

Well maybe we could be needed just a little less. Oh, did I say that out loud? Well since it's out, I do wish sometimes that I was needed a little less. Then I remember that soon I might not be needed at all. Soon my son will make his own breakfast and those mornings when he sat up on the counter and helped me break the eggs and ate a spoonful of 'p-butter' while I cooked will be just a fond memory. Those nights when I sleepily crawled into bed with him after he woke himself up from a nightmare and cuddled until he fell back asleep will be long gone. Those moments when no one could console my daughter, and the instant I picked her up she stopped crying, will only be stories brought up on holidays when the photo albums come out.

There is absolute joy AND pain in being needed... All. The. Time. But that time is much more fleeting than we think. In the moments when your babies and your business are in their infancies, embrace the exhausting fact that you're needed. Your love, sweat, and tears are the only way your babies and business will survive; it's a lot to shoulder, but you've got this.

You might wonder if you'll ever get sleep again, and in the short run the answer might be no. Trust me, you learn to adapt. You might wonder if all of that hard work on your business will pay off, and that answer is a resounding yes. Does that mean that your business will be a wild success, and that your children will grow up to be the next president? Maybe not. The payoff I'm referring to is the lessons you'll learn, the love you'll share, and the amazing adventures you'll remember. There is nothing that will be able to take that away from you. Remember that.

Sometimes all that being needed can get overwhelming, especially in the beginning. It's normal to feel overwhelmed sometimes, remember that it comes in cycles. It's important to pay attention to those bad days. A few bad days in a row are expected, but if you notice that you're having bad weeks, then it's time to get support. The term Postpartum Depression is a serious one, and not to be taken lightly. If you think it could never happen to you, or that it somehow means you aren't a good mother, then stop yourself right there. When you have a baby, there's a lot that's happening to your body in a short amount of time. There are all sorts of things that can happen and you should be on the lookout. You'll be happy you reached out instead of keeping it to yourself, and the Boss Mom community is here to help, and show you that you are not alone.

17

The Art of Seeking Out and Accepting Good Help

Have you ever imagined what you would do if you won the lottery? Pretty much every time the jackpot gets big my husband and I talk about what we would do if we won. If you haven't imagined what you would do with $200 million, then I suggest you take a few moments right now and think about it. It's a wonderful exercise in what you're passionate about, and what you'd give away in a heartbeat.

Maybe you would hire a full-time housekeeper, or a nanny. Maybe you would get more massages and buy more clothes. I bet one thing you wouldn't do is sit there and think about how you should continue do everything yourself. With that kind of money you would hire a full staff to help take the burden of everyday living off of your hands. If you had the money you wouldn't even have to think twice to get good help, right? So why are you refusing to get the support you need right now? Why do I assume you are refusing good support?

Well it's a hunch, but a well-founded one for sure.

ACCEPTING GOOD HELP

Pretty much every Boss Mom I know at some point or another thinks she has to be all things to all people. If it's in the mom department, then we try to show that we can cook, clean, teach, feed, and love... all simultaneously. Oh, and while wearing heels and makeup. I don't know a single woman who can do all of that. Now don't get me wrong, there are times when we do it all, but it's not sustainable. Or maybe you're the mom who said goodbye to the idea of heels and choreographed meals a long time ago. I say in all things moderation.

The issue doesn't lie in what we can do, the issue lies in our preconceived notion of what we SHOULD be able to do. All those times when I was pregnant and people offered to help me with my groceries. I thought to myself, well I 'can' carry them myself, therefore I 'should' carry them myself. I remember a good friend who would decline help by saying, "that's ok, I've got hands". But the point of offering up help wasn't because she couldn't do it herself, the point was that it would make getting it done easier for her, and that's what I wanted, I wanted to help make her life just a little easier.

When it comes to help we all too often feel guilty that we're adding undue burden in people's lives by allowing them to help us, but it's not burdensome to help the ones we love. That person at the grocery store that offered to help, they probably have kids at home and remember all too well the challenges you face ahead. Accept their help. That colleague who wants to help review that marketing email you're about to send out, they probably remember the glitches that happened when they send out their first marketing email. Accept their help.

The sooner you realize that you need all of the help you can get, and that it in no way reflects on your ability to run your own life, the sooner you will find yourself moving forward. Let people help you, and when it's time, you can repay the universe by helping someone else. I'm sure you've heard of the term 'pay it forward', well, that can be a great substitute for guilt. Just image a time in the future when you can offer up the same gracious assistance that you're getting now. You'll be able to spot when it's the right time to give back. It may take the form of washing dishes, carrying groceries, changing diapers, reviewing content, giving feedback, or being a mentor. You'll know because you will see an opportunity to help someone get through it (whatever 'it' is) just a little bit easier than you did. You'll feel empathy rise up into your heart and at that moment you will fully understand how helping those we care about is not a burden, but a joy.

SEEKING OUT GOOD HELP

There will be times when there's no one around to offer up support in certain areas of your life, even when you really need the help. Sometimes the timing just doesn't work out in your favor, but don't be discouraged, there are lots of ways to seek out good help.

Here are some tips from the Boss Mom community on how to find the support you need:

1. **REACH OUT TO COMMUNITIES** like the Boss Mom Facebook group, other online groups, your Church, other moms or entrepreneurs in your community, or meet-ups. Ask if people have experience with your particular situation and if they have suggestions, or a resource they can recommend. You might be surprised at how much sharing and support you can get when you ask people for their guidance.

2. **THINK ABOUT SWAPPING SERVICES OR KIDS**. Almost every entrepreneur I know has done a service swap at some point in their career. Reach out to your community and let them know where you need help and what value you bring to the table. There are tons of entrepreneurs out there who would love to swap services to keep their costs down. When it comes to your kids you can always try a babysitting swap or co-op. This is where a group of moms take turns watching the kids to help each other out. There's a great blog post by the Frugal Mama on this topic that you can check out at www.frugal-mama.com.

3. **OPEN UP A 'JOB POSITION'** for whatever it is you need and put it up on your website or post about it. Just because it isn't full time, or you just want to hire a consultant, coach, or VA, doesn't mean you can't position

it as an open spot on your team. This allows you to take applications and have a little more of a process to help you make the right decision for you and your business. These are just a few ways to find the support you need.

Ultimately the first step is to accept that you need the help in the first place. Now that you're a mom and an entrepreneur you have very little extra time to waste, and getting stressed out and overworked can just cause more wasted time. Those around you can see that you are doing amazing things in this world. You're creating life in your family and in your business, and people want to help see that flourish. So if you have a hard time taking a helping hand, I want you to stand in front of the mirror and say this: The next time someone offers to help me, I'll accept with an open heart, because I know that they are giving out of love, and I can always use more love in my life.

18

Flex Scheduling: How to Block Your Time When You Have a Baby & a Business

When it comes to babies and businesses, the one issue that constantly comes up is time. When your priorities follow your passions you always wish you had more time, and why wouldn't you? A good friend of mine said that she would stay up after the kids went to sleep to get work done and actually had to make herself go to bed because she enjoyed what she was doing. She often regretted it in the morning when her kids would spring out of bed at 5:30am. I've done the same thing from time to time, how about you?

The simple truth is that no matter how well we set our priorities each day, we will always wish we had more time if we're doing what we love. So let's stop thinking about each day as a certain allotment of time. I had a client once who told me she got so angry with herself at the end of each day because she didn't check everything off her to-do list. She had her kids at home and since their needs were never on a set schedule, it was hard for her to get into the zone and get things done. So her list just sat there half the time. She would stare at it not knowing where to start. So, thinking about that dilemma, I invented my own version of flex scheduling. Since then I've implemented it in my life and I have to admit that it really works; not just to manage time, but to keep me positive and motivated too.

So what exactly is flex scheduling? Simply put, it's all about blocking categories of time. Instead of having that massive and scary to-do list, you create blocks of time that meet certain criteria. The categories might not be what you think. Instead of thinking about the 'types' of tasks you have to complete, maybe client, marketing, or admin, the categories are set up based on how much mental strength you need to complete the task. When you block your to-do list in this way it allows you to shift your tasks each day according to your current situation. Maybe your kids wake up early from their nap and you stop working to make their lunch and get them set up to eat. Once they're eating you still need to keep an eye on them, but they don't need constant attention, that's a yellow category, or medium mental strength needed. You might be able to engage in a Facebook group during this time, set up your schedule for the week, prep dinner, or do some stretching. This might not be a good time to get immersed in a client project, or write your next blog or book, even if that was what you were doing when they were napping.

The key with flex scheduling is that it helps you have a

pool of tasks you can tackle no matter what life throws your way. This helps keep you focused and positive. You can feel like you're still getting things accomplished, even when the day didn't go exactly as planned.

The first thing to do when setting up your flex schedule is to create 3 category buckets. You can do this on a sheet of paper, create color categories in your online scheduler, or download our flex scheduler at www.boss-mom.com/BMBresources. Your three categories are 'little attention', 'some attention', and 'full attention'. Feel free to name these however you want, but the main idea is that each one is a varied level of mental presence.

Now start to look at your daily tasks and place them in a bucket. I bet you haven't looked at your tasks in this way before. Are you surprised at how many tasks you have in a particular bucket? I know I was. I had to get really honest with myself and acknowledge when I was putting something in the little attention because I 'could' do it without really paying attention, but I found that I really wasn't able to do it well without fulling paying attention. Just going through this simple exercise can help you see where you might be sabotaging your ability to do your best work.

Now that you have all of your daily tasks in one of these three buckets you're set to create your schedule. If you have kids at home and you know you get a certain amount of time when they're napping, then make sure your full attention items are slotted in at that time. If you know that you work best in the morning then make sure to schedule your full attention items first thing. Now when something unexpected happens, you can look at your buckets and quickly see what you can still tackle.

If you want to take it a step further, then jot down your estimated commitment time and note if there's a hard due date. Now you can look at your buckets and easily see where you might fit something in when your kids fall asleep in the car, or when you happen to arrive at a meeting 20 minutes early.

Flex scheduling isn't meant to replace your current calendar system, it's meant to augment it in a way that helps you get more done, and feel more productive too. As Boss Moms we get a lot thrown our way, often from left field, and that means we struggle to shift things around in our schedule to make it all work. Now you can easily move things around and fill your time when you have it.

I guess you could say there's a fourth bucket too. That's the 'turn everything off and enjoy your family and you time' bucket. You don't really have to put anything in particular in this bucket, but you should know it exists. My mornings are my fourth bucket time. I'm with my kids with all of my heart and soul each and every morning. No meetings, no social media, nothing, just a lot of giggles and hugs. Decide when your fourth bucket time will be and enjoy every second.

TIME SENSITIVE & PRIORITY PROJECTS

What do you do when you have project deadlines and

your kid gets sick... or maybe you get sick? What do you do about your schedule then? This is a dilemma I hear all the time. Pretty much every mom out there has run into this at one point or another and I'm amazed at how much guilt we feel when we can't get everything done at once. There is just no way to take care of your sick kid and get in a full day's work too. Even if you try to squeeze some work in, you may find that your poor, feverish kid who wants nothing but your hugs all day long will keep you from physically or mentally getting good work done.

There is no simple answer to this one, but I will say this: life happens. We don't live in a vacuum where everything is always perfect, no one gets sick, and nothing ever breaks down. Things happen that can veer us off course and there's nothing to feel guilty about. If you're a parent and your clients don't understand that if you get a call from daycare you're going to drop everything and pick your child up right away, then you might be working with the wrong people. **THE KEY ISN'T TO TRY AVOID EVER HAVING UNEXPECTED THINGS HAPPEN IN YOUR LIFE, THE KEY IS TO WORK WITH PEOPLE WHO EMPATHIZE WITH YOUR LIFE'S CHALLENGES AND PRIORITIES.**

When you only work with people who align with your life priorities, then all of a sudden you don't get that sinking feeling in your soul when you have to call and cancel a meeting because your child needs you. You already know that your client will understand and most of the time they'll tell you it's not a problem, and in fact, they might mention that a few weeks back they had to move a meeting for the very same reason. And when you have aligned priorities with your clients, then it's easier to communicate when a deadline is truly pressing. This allows you to know when you really need to push and put in a few late nights, and when it's ok to just stop everything for a day or two. It's not a foolproof solution, but I can keep you from unnecessarily spinning your wheels, and that can be positively powerful.

The interesting thing about scheduling is that it isn't just about the tasks that need to be done each day. Scheduling is about recognizing who's in your life, how you feel, and what moves you. **SCHEDULING IS ALMOST AN ART FORM WHERE YOU WORK TO EXTRACT MAXIMUM RESULTS, OUT OF LIMITED TIME**. Your scheduling should be less about allocating your time, and more about seeing how much you accomplish. The more you look at your schedule in this way, the more you'll get done, and the better you'll feel about what you accomplish each day.

PART 6: THE FIRST YEAR
Your Baby's and Business' Infancy

19

The Best-Laid Plans: Adjusting to Your Changing Baby's (and Business') Routine

We are creatures of habit. There's a sense of comfort from knowing what's coming next, and most of us enjoy a well-established routine when we are able to put one in place. Unfortunately, when it comes to businesses and babies, you shouldn't get too comfortable. Once you take the leap to become a mother and an entrepreneur you enter into a territory of constant change, and it can have some bumpy terrain.

Even though change is inevitable, you should still seek out positive routines and just realize from the start that at some point those routines will change. All of the change you will experience is due to the fact that your baby and your business is growing. At each stage of their life they will have new needs, learn new things, and engage with you in new ways.

Now that I have two "littles", I find myself saying that I thought having a baby was difficult, until I had a toddler, and now I realize how easy a baby can be. I have a feeling I'll be saying the same thing when my kids hit the teen years. As my son grows I'm constantly surprised at how much he changes each day, and sometimes he takes great leaps that are truly amazing. There will be days when your baby has a growth spurt, eats all day long, and actually wakes up the next day taller. How crazy is that?

Did you know your business can wake up taller too? Oh yeah, your business will go through just as many changes and growth spurts as your kids. Every day you'll wake up and be amazed at all of the new things your business is doing and saying. You'll be amazed at the new friends your business makes, the new things your business needs each month to stay fulfilled, and how often it grows out of different tools as it starts to grow up.

Pretty much the second you really get comfortable is when a big change is inevitably coming down the pike. Embrace it. These changes are challenging and can sometimes come by total surprise in the middle of the night. When this happens you should pull them close, adjust, and help them grow.

The hard thing to realize is that they didn't ask to change and grow. They are like flowers in your garden that you choose to nourish. They don't know why they reach for the sun, they only know that you have provided all they need to allow them to grow. It's a beautiful blessing to watch something you love change into something amazing and beautiful.

What holds us back and causes unnecessary stress and

frustration is this tug-of-war between being organized and embracing change. How can you have processes set in place if everything is just going to change on you? What you have to realize is that a good process and routine are what help your baby and business grow, and that growth causes change. It's a sort of catch-22, an inevitable cycle that's at the very root of your ability to grow a thriving business and family.

Acceptance of this cycle has amazingly positive effects. Spend time organizing your business; those efficiencies are what will free up your time to bring in more clients. Spend time settling your children into good routines, it's what gives them the confidence and structure to blossom into the next stages of life. And when those growing pains begin you can take a deep breath and jump right in to start a new routine and a new process. Each time this happens you're creating a stepping stone to lift you, your baby, and your business up and help move you forward.

20

Momarazzi:
Making Time to Document Your Journey

I bet you have no problem taking countless pictures of your children, dog, outfits, flowers, or whatever else you enjoy and love most. How many of those pictures have you actually organized into a photo album? Could you go into your phone or computer and easily walk through a timeline of your child's life so far?

We have the best intentions, but we get busy, and those amazing photos start to digitally stack up in a proverbial storage closet. Dust begins to collect and we start to forget that we took that picture because it was the first time they did that one thing that was so adorable. What was that one thing again? I can't remember because I didn't write it down, I just took a picture and assumed I would always know.

When my son was born I catalogued so many moments with photos and journals. Every 3 months I would pull everything together and print a photo album. If you look on my book shelf you'll see a set of beautiful albums that go all the way to 9 months old. The problem is that my son is 2 already. I still have hundreds of photos from the last 15 months all housed in a nice set of folders, but that's the problem, they're just sitting there. Why? Because I haven't had time to sit down and put more albums together. Ok, let's be honest, I haven't made time to put them together; it just seems so much more important to live in the present and prepare for the future than to catalogue the past.

There's a flaw in this thinking. Sure we should be present as much as possible. Sure we should be looking to the future as we build our family and business. But the past offers something oh-so-very important; it offers us memories and those memories can be a powerful thing.

One of my favorite children's movies is the 'Rise of the Guardians' by director Peter Ramsey. It's this great story with this wonderful band of classic characters like Santa Clause, the Easter Bunny, the Tooth Fairy, Sandman, and Jack Frost. They guard the children and their childlike wonder, but in the movie Pitch Black (ie, the Boogie Man) threatens their survival by trying to get the children to stop believing. At one point he steals the children's teeth from the Tooth Palace and you find out that the reason they collect the teeth is because they hold important memories. When a child needs help remembering what's important the Tooth Fairy uses the memories from their lost teeth to help them remember. Ok, that sounds a lot creepier than it actually is in the movie. It's quite endearing, and as you watch you think back to those amazing memories from your childhood and this warmth just floods your heart.

MEMORIES HAVE THE POWER TO REMIND US OF WHAT'S IMPORTANT. They have the power to guide us back to our path. They have the ability to shift our emotions back to love and compassion. Memories are important, and unless we spend the time to put them somewhere where we can easily access them, we run the risk of them getting lost. Our memories are too important to risk, so when you think you're too busy to spend time on your memories, stop and remember just how much you have to lose.

YOUR BUSINESS JOURNEY

Your business memories are important too. Those first renditions of your website are an important part of your past and your journey. Each time you redesign, rethink, redo, you are moving closer to your 'why' and your purpose. Each time you decide your brand needs a revamp it's because you realize how it can be better, and more impactful.

We tend to simply design over our past renditions of our business like a painter reusing a canvas, and we often lose our ability to look back. Those past blog posts, logos, sales pages, and presentations, are all testaments to how much you, and your business, have changed and grown. Don't deny yourself the ability to look back and see how much you have accomplished.

The next time you decide to make a change to your business, think about what you will be changing and whether you can document what it looks like now. Take a screen shot of your website pages, save that old version of your 'about' page, file away one of those old business cards. You may be eager to get rid of them in the moment, but you'll be thankful you saved them when you try to laughingly tell someone about how archaic your first logo looked. And you will be able to come home and pull that old business card out and smile.

21

Is Your Baby and Business Really That Cute?

Many a parent have sat for hours on end just staring at their baby. They watch with love and wonder as their baby does the same thing over and over again. I know because I've done it, and every single person I know that has kids has done it too. On a daily basis I turn to my husband and exclaim that I love my kids so much I feel like I'm going to burst. He just grins and shakes his head. Ironically, my daughter actually woke up while writing this chapter and I took a break to feed her and couldn't stop staring. She fell asleep in my arms and I just sat there caressing her cheek with my finger. I had to force myself to put her back in her crib.

As parents we take countless pictures and send them to everyone we know to show them just how adorable our children are. Everyone thinks their baby is the cutest baby that ever existed. We can't help ourselves. We peer into our baby's eyes and see absolute adorableness. Even when they cry or scream, we still see that cuteness shining through. Ok, most of the time.

But not every baby is the cutest baby in the world, right? Of course not. But that's the brilliance of it all. It doesn't matter whether the world thinks your baby is cute or not, what matters is what YOU see.

You know they say love is blind, but I think love lets you see. Of course you look at your child and see only beauty, they are a part of you. I didn't notice just how chubby my son was until I looked back at his 3 month pictures and realized he looked like a big marshmallow. All I saw was absolute love. It didn't make him any skinnier or change who he was, but it did change how I saw him. The brilliant thing about absolute love is that it allows us to have total acceptance without judgement. We see beauty because we accept everything about them. Their so-called flaws are smoothed over with our love, and all we see is love's light beaming through.

Your business has that power too. Tell me you haven't caught yourself re-reading a blog post you wrote, continually glancing at your new logo, or shared a client review with everyone you know. You look at your business with that same love and awe. You see the beauty in your business because it's your baby.

You look at your business and baby and think they're the cutest thing that ever existed, and you're right. To you that statement is the absolute truth, and that's all that matters. That beauty that you see is love personified; its love shining through you onto the one you love and bouncing back radiant light. This light is what helps you see your way when times get tough.

So don't ever question just how cute your business or your baby is, beauty is a perception, and yours is the only one that matters.

22

The Crying Baby: Recognizing What You Can Do and Letting Go of the Rest

Around week 4 your baby starts crying. Nothing you do seems to help and you feel as though they've been crying for days. You search the internet for everything you can think of in hopes that it will at least confirm that something is wrong, because imaging that this screaming child is just your normal baby is a scary thought. You touch their head and decide it feels hot so you immediately take them to the doctor. The doctor tells you they're fine and that this is just a phase all babies go through. You go home stressed out, but at least now you know you can't really fix the issue, all you can do is love your baby until they get better.

There will be times in the life of your baby and business when you just can't help. There will be times when they hurt, feel sad, or feel angry, and there will be nothing you can do to make them feel better. You try and try, but at some point there's an opportunity cost to trying to fix something that can't

129

be fixed. That opportunity cost is your sanity. It's painful and frustrating to not be able to fix something you love, but not letting go can cause some serious damage over the long haul.

It's not always easy to recognize the tipping point where you should stop, step back, and take yourself out of the equation. Part of you feels like if you give up now, then it somehow says you don't love your baby or you aren't committed enough to your business. This nagging feeling is like the snake in the Garden, it whispers into your ear and causes you to unnecessarily doubt yourself. You know you're a loving, wonderful mom, and walking away and letting your baby cry won't change that. In fact, sometimes that's the best thing to do.

WHEN TO HELP

I think it goes without saying that us Boss Moms will always put in the effort and work to help make our baby and business happy. It's an instinct that's planted inside of us. It's part of our nature to nurture.

I have a good friend and colleague who openly questions whether she will be a good mother. She mentions how she just isn't that great with kids and is so committed to her business that she worries she won't be committed enough to her baby. The thing is, she WANTS to be a mom. She wants it bad, but this feeling she gets holds her back. Every time we talk about it I mention all of the wonderful things she does that proves she is loving and nurturing. This fear that we won't be loving enough is more common than you think, and it's also a completely unfounded fear. You will be, and are, an amazingly loving and nurturing mom. You might make mistakes here and here, we all do, but you have an immense amount of love to give; never question that.

When your baby and business start to cry here's a good rundown scenario of what to do.

1   **DO A QUICK ASSESSMENT**. Is your baby hungry, do they need to be changed, or burped? Is your business hungry for new clients, do they need a little brand change, or copy altered? There's a short list of possible common problems that you can run through to see if you can quickly find the right solution.

2   If that fails, then step two is to **DO A LITTLE RESEARCH**. Ask people you know and trust if they have encountered this particular situation. What did they do? Sometimes outside experience and perspective is all you need to help resolve an issue. You can always hop on a search engine and see what comes up, but be aware that this can cause unneeded panic. Too many moms have been thrown into a fit of despair thinking their child had some rare lethal rash because they searched the internet and found something that 'might' look like what their kid has. I believe you should always err on the side of caution though, and when in doubt go to the doctor or hospital.

3   Finally, **IF YOU DECIDE ACTION IS NEEDED**, then don't hesitate to hop in the car and make a visit to Urgent

Care. Don't be afraid to pull out your emergency call and talk to your business coach. You'll know when something is truly urgent, and since you've gone through step one and two, you can be confident it's the right choice.

WHEN TO LET GO

After you've gone through this whole process and decided that there is no real solution at this time, then allow yourself to sit down for a second and breath. Odds are you've been in a constant state of panic this whole time. You're tense and stressed and that will only make it harder to make rational decisions and be there for your family and business. So take a few minutes and instead of trying to fix it, just be there. Offer up love and support by holding your baby close, or maybe walking away for a little bit to let your baby reset. Be there for your business by letting the frustration (that your website is having issues) go, and pay positive attention to a part of your business that is doing well.

Sometimes, both your baby and your business need you to just be there. I know it can be hard to not jump in and try to save the day, but your role as a mom and entrepreneur isn't always to be the savior. Sometimes that role goes to someone else, or maybe time will resolve the issue. Once you accept this and allow it to sink in, then you can recognize when it's time to let go and when it's time to take action. Your soul and muscles will thank you.

23

Troubleshooting: How to Assess and Be Agile

Ever since you started your own business I bet there are two words that you don't hear yourself say anymore. Any guesses? Its Politics and Red Tape. Ok red tape is two words, but it's one phrase so it counts. There's a very good reason why you don't use these words anymore. You are now your own boss, so you get to decide who you work with and how you run your business. That means you don't have to work with people who don't mesh well with you, and you don't have to sit around hoping someone will approve changes in your business.

How liberating. You get to decide what exactly will happen in your business on a day to day basis. That sounds amazing until things stop working and you find yourself in uncharted territory. Running your own business can be scary, and it can also mean a lot of troubleshooting, also known as trial and error, or (as I like to call it) 'why don't we try this'.

Remember those 3 steps you take when your business

starts to cry? You assess, research and take action. The action you take is completely up to you, but the beauty of being the boss, or Boss Mom, is that you have the ability to be as agile as you want to be in your business. You want to add a new service, go right ahead. You want to completely rebrand, do it. You want to shut down your 12k member Facebook group because it no longer fits with your goals, shut it down (I actually know someone who did this). The point is that you can do anything you want in your business, you have that power.

All that power is usually accompanied by the fear that you might not always be making the right decisions for your business. The simple solution is to have a support team that can help you with your decisions so that you can confidently make quick changes in your business as needed. There are three great ways to get the mental support you need.

⚲ **GET A BUSINESS COACH.** No matter how successful you get, everyone could use a coach to act as a sounding board. Your coach should be someone you trust and enjoy. This will be someone who you can be brutally honest with when it comes to the state of your business. They need to be someone who you will listen to and can hold you accountable. You can exchange services or hire one, but find someone that feels right. This person will be able to help you make big decisions for your business, and help create the confidence you need to remove barriers and continue to move forward.

2 **JOIN A MASTERMIND**. While your coach should be someone who has more experience and knowledge than you, a mastermind group should be made up of people that are all at a similar state in their career. This is a group that has different areas of expertise. Just like your coach, everyone should feel comfortable around each other, and respect each other's expertise and perspective. You can join a paid mastermind, or you can reach out to women, or men, in your community and ask if they want to create a mastermind with you. Either way, the group should meet in person, or virtually, at least one a month, and talk through each other's wins and challenges. This is an excellent way to get multiple perspectives on important decisions.

3 **REACH OUT TO YOUR COMMUNITY**. If you're making a decision about your brand, services or products, then you should consider asking your community before you act. Reach out to your email list, Facebook group, or social media following and ask them what they think. An effective approach is to give them several options and ask which one they like best. So give your community three logo ideas, three product names, or three color options and see what they say. This is a great way to see what will truly resonate with your ideal client, and it might not always be what you expected. By the way, the title,

subtitle, and book cover for this book were all selected by the Boss Mom community.

Having the support you need will make it that much easier to assess your business, be agile and take action. This means you can change as your industry changes, and you can change as you and your family changes. Remember that you have that power. The moment you don't want to get up and go to work, make sure you assess why, and then make a change. **YOU SHOULD BE PASSIONATE ABOUT WHAT YOU DO, YOU EARNED THAT RIGHT WHEN YOU DECIDED TO BE BRAVE AND BECOME AN ENTREPRENEUR.**

PART 7: TODDLER TIME

Helping Your Baby and Business Grow

24

Is Your Baby & Business Teething?

You made it. You have a business and a family, and you're watching them grow. You've gotten through some of those tough times and come out thriving. You rock. Then you realize that there are a lot more challenges coming your way. Now it's time for your business and your baby to really grow, and grow fast.

If you already have toddlers, then you know how horrifying an emerging molar can be for the whole family. Your kid screams in absolute pain at all hours. You know exactly what the issue is, and in order to get everyone comfortable again there might need to be some serious adjusting going on. We're talking co-sleeping, lots of over-the-counter fever reducers (in the proper dosage of course), or toy buying. Well your business might be teething too, and it can be just as scary. While this time in your life can feel hectic, there are ways to help get your sanity back.

THE TEETHING TODDLER

When your kids are in pain, you feel it too. It's heart-wrenching to see our children hurting, and you'll consider trying anything to help them feel better. You might try the OTC meds, or homeopathic teething tablets or even a chilled teething toy, and odds are they will work in some capacity or another. There are countless articles out there (thank goodness!) that can tell you ways to help your teething toddler. I want to help you feel like you are not only dulling the pain, but also that you're helping them understand what's actually happening.

Open your mouth, really wide, and say ahhh. Let your kid see your teeth. Let them touch them, and then let them run their fingers over their own gums and teeth. You can create a game that helps them understand where the pain is coming from. You might be surprised at how much your children pick up if you just start explaining everything. Count their teeth, maybe even name them. I'm a big fan of giving things a name. Tell them that Frank (I like simple names) is trying to grow so that they can chew their food. Then show them what chewing looks like. Engaging your toddler in this way won't make the pain go away, although I think it does help distract them, but it can help them feel less confused about what's going on.

Now when your child is in pain, they know just how to tell you what it is, and that kind of communication can make all of the difference. I encourage you to give it a try and see if it works for you.

THE TEETHING BUSINESS

If you're lucky, your business will experience this kind of growth. It may feel painful at the time, but teething is a good sign that you are doing something right. The thing to remember with a teething business is that as each tooth comes in your opening up new possibilities.

Just like how a teething toddler now has more food options, will most likely take up biting, and will now have to learn to brush their teeth, your teething business may also notice positive and negative changes. As your business grows you might experience increased pricing and a new kind of client. You might outgrow certain tools and have to learn all new ones. You might even get more business than you can handle and have to figure out how to adjust. These are all very real possibilities and some can be hard to manage.

As these changes happen, make sure that you help foster good communication with your community, just like you did with your toddler. They might be feeling the pains of your growth too. It might be a breakdown in the client experience, or you might begin to transition away from certain clients all together. Be conscious of what's causing the growth, and how it will affect everything around you. This will help you create smoother transitions as you grow.

The most common growing pain that I've seen among Boss Moms with growing businesses, is how quickly your business can take over your life and pull you away from your family. We all want to be successful in whatever we do, but as Boss Moms we also want to create a life we love. Once you start to establish yourself and your business, you'll start to get more clients, and sell more products, until one day you find yourself staying up late every night just to keep up. You still love what you do, but you find yourself drowning with no life raft in site.

As soon as you start to see your business grow, put a few safety measures in place. Now is a good time to go back to chapter 10 and think about how you'll prepare your business for this growth. Even though your income may be going up, fight the urge to go on a shopping spree just yet. In order to ensure you aren't up all hours trying to run your business, you will most likely need to bring on more support, and that costs money. Revisit your business budget and plug in a few numbers to see what it would look like if you were getting extra help.

This is also a good time to reassess and decide how much you really WANT to grow. Depending on what you do, you might want to build an international empire with hundreds of employees. Or maybe you never intended on working full time again, and just want a small side business that brings in extra cash for the family. Both routes, and everything in between, are ok. Choose whichever path is right for you. Don't let anyone tell you how you should grow your business. If you don't want to get bigger, then you can make the choice to stop growing and stay small. There are plenty of very happy Boss Moms out there that have done just that. Following what feels right for you and your life, will ensure you continue to love your business at every stage.

25

The Art of Saying No Like Your Kids Do

Kids have this hilarious and frustrating ability to say 'no' with total ease and gusto. My son tilts his head and adorably says 'no mommy'. Sometimes it's an appropriate 'no' and sometimes we have to explain that you can't always say no to mommy. That's usually when we cringe for a moment wondering if this will be the time he decides to have a complete meltdown. I mean arms flailing, massive tears, snot everywhere, high-pitched yelling… the works. I realize that he says no with such enthusiasm because he just recently became conscious of his own opinions and his ability to express himself to get what he wants. What an amazing feeling that must be. You have to appreciate the fact that kids know what they want and are willing to fight for it, like literally fight for it.

SAYING YES TOO OFTEN

As Boss Moms we say yes a lot. I think we feel like we have to. Things need to be taken care of and who else is going to do it, right? Well in our business that shouldn't be the case. My Digital Strategist, podcast co-host, and dear friend, NJ Rongner, said something on our podcast once that changed my world. She said that it's a lot easier to turn a 'no' into a 'yes' than it is to take a 'yes' back. She also talked about how every time she says 'no' she thinks about everything she just said yes to. I really love that way of thinking.

It can be really hard to say no in our business, or just life in general. When it comes to our business we want to see it flourish and in the beginning we think that saying yes to everything is the only way to help it grow. As we begin to establish ourselves, we start to realize that saying yes to everyone doesn't help anyone. You want to do what you do best, and remember that even though you can do something, that doesn't mean you should.

If you have a hard time saying no don't fret, there are some easy techniques you can use to help get more comfortable with gracefully declining things that just don't fit with your overall goals. There are a few reasons you would say no to a possible client, opportunity, or collaboration. Either you don't have time, they aren't aligned with your overall goals, or the timing just isn't right.

If you don't have time, then saying no can get a lot easier, but you also want to consider whether you would have said yes if you had the time. This is an important question to ask because you may want to leave a door open to work together in the future as time permits. Or maybe you let them know when you would be available; sometimes your ideal client is willing to wait for you.

If they aren't aligned with your overall goals, then don't hesitate to say no, but also acknowledge that they may be perfectly aligned with someone else's goals. If you know someone who would be a better fit, then make an introduction. Even though you said no, you will be leaving a positive impression.

Sometimes the stars just don't align and that conference, collaboration, or project just doesn't make sense. Maybe you're expecting and the thought of planning to speak at a conference a few months after the little one arrives will cause more stress than good. Maybe you want to work with the person, but the proposed project just doesn't fit with what you're doing in your business right now. This is where you say no, but let them know that you look forward to the right opportunity in the future.

If you aren't sure what to say when it comes time to say no, then spend a little time now writing out a few scripts. Write one for each of these three scenarios. They don't have to be exactly what you say when the times comes, but writing them out now will help give you the words you need to confidently say no with grace and gusto.

26

Be the Bow: Let Their Personalities Shine

We give so much to our children that sometimes it's hard to remember that they are their own person that will grow up and live their own life someday. In The Prophet, by Kahlil Gibran, he speaks of our children and says, "They come through you but not from you, and though they are with you yet they belong not to you." IT'S A BEAUTIFUL REMINDER THAT EVEN THOUGH WE SPENT NINE MONTHS CREATING LIFE, AND SO MANY YEARS SACRIFICING SLEEP AND A BIT OF SANITY TO HELP OUR CHILDREN GROW, THEY ARE NOT OURS TO KEEP.

The Prophet goes on to say something truly powerful. He says, "You are the bows from which your children as living arrows are sent forth. The archer sees the mark upon the path of the infinite, and He bends you with His might that His arrows may go swift and far." When my parents first introduced me to this book so many years ago, they signed it saying, "may you go swift and far". Funny, looking back now

147

I see that not only was it a beautiful inscription, it was also an unconscious testament to their parenting.

As parents we have an obligation to our children. We have an obligation to show them what love looks like, to help them nourish their bodies, and learn how to engage with the world. Everything we do for our children is in the hope that the foundation we set is strong enough to keep them steady when times get tough. We hope that they grow up to make good decisions and lead a happy and fulfilled life. And whether we admit it or not, I think we also want to be able to do a little victory dance to celebrate that we did a good job as parents.

We are the bow and our children are the arrows. We can be strong and steady, and as soon as we set that arrow flying then we have to realize that our children hold the power to stay on course or waver. We may agonizingly watch them falter, and odds are at some point they will. No kid or adult is perfect. I know I had a few moments as a kid and a young adult that terrified my parents, and I have no doubt that my children will have some of those moments too. The thing to remember is that we are their support, not their crutch. We are here to help set them on the path, not hold their hand. When we step back we allow our children's personality to shine; we give them the freedom to be who they want to be.

This advice applies to your business as well. Your brand has a personality of its own. We tend to create a brand that represents us, but sometimes our brand is so much more than just us. Allow yourself to be the bow that sets your business on the right course, and then listen and allow your businesses personality to shine.

In the end, it's hard to tell exactly how our family and business will turn out, but I hope with all my heart that both go swift and far.

27

Little Ones Have Big Ears: Your Child and Business are Smarter Than You Think

You might not realize your children are listening until they repeat something you didn't want repeated. I know my husband and I have become super conscious of saying that occasional cuss word and we spell out certain words like 'pool' and 'pizza' so we don't have to hear our son repeat those words for an hour. We might not think that our kids are paying attention to what we say and do, but they're often a lot smarter than we think.

Our children are like sponges just waiting to soak up everything we throw their way. Especially in those first few years, they are built to take everything in and learn as much as possible. We work hard to teach them how to use a spoon, say 'mama', and count to five, but we often miss all of the other things we're teaching our kids.

Everything you do is an example for your kids. Now that's a scary thought, but it's so true. They see the way we treat other people, the way we handle situations, the way we experience the world. Our every action is a powerful lesson on how they should act, and that can have a powerful impact.

Have you ever been frustrated, tired or angry and without even uttering a word, you notice that your child, spouse or colleague has suddenly become defensive or upset? I remember having a run-in with a new car seat a few years back. I am happy to say that I finally figured the darned thing out, but it left me frustrated. I took that mood home with me and when I picked up my 5 month old son he immediately started to fidget and whine, which didn't help my mood. When I handed him over to my husband, he was almost instantly happy again. That was the moment I realized that I wasn't the only one being affected by my bad mood.

Now 'Mood Transfer' as I like to call it, isn't a new idea. In 1993 Elaine Hatfield, John Cacioppo, and Richard Rapson published a now classic book called, 'Emotional Contagion'. Put simply, the authors provide evidence that shows that our emotions are communicated to others even when we try to hide them. And here's the important point: Our mannerisms give us away, and our emotions are contagious. The tone of our voice, the way we move, and the words we use all affect those around us, whether we want them to or not. My mood affected my son, just like your mood can affect your friends, family and clients.

Realizing this, I closed my eyes and took a deep breath. Then I picked my son up and gave him a big hug and kiss and told him I loved him. He giggled. My mood suddenly changed and happily, so did his. And as a bonus, my husband's mood changed too, from defensive, to calm and happy. Once I saw how quickly I was able to change the mood dynamic in my family, I began to wonder how many times I could have created a more positive, productive environment by simply changing my mood.

Now I realize we can't always give a big hug and kiss to a colleague or client and make it all better, but there are a few things we can do to help us see things in a more positive light.

1   **TAKE A DEEP BREATH**: Don't pass over this one. It is one of the most effective ways to calm down. Deep breathing stimulates the parasympathetic nervous system, which helps to lower your blood pressure and heart rate and helps you relax.

2   **RECOUNT A HAPPY STORY OR IMAGINE SOMETHING GREAT HAPPENING**: Richard Boyatzis and his colleagues at Case Western Reserve University have researched and studied how talking about positive events and aspirations have a positive effect on the brain. It turns out that PEAs (Positive Emotional Attractors) can significantly affect mood and motivation. Don't underestimate the power of a happy memory or dreams of a better tomorrow!

3   **GIVE A COMPLIMENT**: Did you ever notice that when you're in a bad mood, you are focused on yourself. When you step back and consciously take a look at others in

order to offer a compliment, it can help get you out of the rut of thinking about whatever it is that is bothering you. And beyond the good of giving a compliment, the response you get is often enough to set you right again.

Bear in mind that not all bad moods can be cured with a simple exercise. If you just can't shake it, talk to someone you trust about what's bothering you, or meet with a professional counselor.

Ultimately we all want to be happy, and finding ways to stay positive can act as a ripple effect out into the world. Find ways each day to set your positive intentions out into the world, and then live those intentions. You never know when your positive energy is changing lives for the better, especially your babies and business.

28

Is Her Kid Smarter Than Mine?
The Terrible Trap of Comparison

I remember seeing a YouTube video a friend posted of her twelve month old daughter counting to ten. For weeks my husband feverishly tried to teach our son to count, to no avail. I think we can all agree that counting at twelve months is a pretty amazing accomplishment. It was amazing that her daughter could do that, but the fact that our son couldn't didn't mean there was something wrong.

We get caught in this trap all of the time in business too, we see someone have a huge launch and we begin to wonder why we're in business at all since we haven't been able to accomplish those same results. It's great to look at how others have found success and see how we can mimic some of the tactics that fit well with our goals, but holding ourselves to their level of achievement isn't going to help us get where we want to go.

YOUR KID IS AWESOME

Here's the facts. Odds are your child won't be a savant in every aspect of their life. They'll be great at some things and not so great at others. They'll beam with light in certain areas and fall asleep with boredom in others. Just like you, they were never built to be all things to all people.

Your job isn't to make them brilliant at everything, your job is to help them discover what their good at, and what makes them happy. My son is just now learning to count at two years old. That's just fine with me, because he can climb like a five year old, is already saying full sentences, and is an overall happy kid. The things he loves are the things we foster, and the places where he needs a little extra help, we provide support, but don't push to the level of frustration. He'll get there and we celebrate the wins, even if they might be a little later than other kids.

Instead of spending time looking at what other kids are doing, look at your kid. They will give you signs all day long about what they are good at; you just have to see past the task and find the behavior. What does that mean? It just means that if your kid loves to do things the same way every time, then maybe they enjoy process. If your kid likes to put the train tracks together a different way each time, then maybe they like the creative process of change. These can be great indicators of what your kid might like to do, and can help you test out different games and hobbies. I'm no child psychologist, so I make a full disclaimer that thinking in behaviors and not just tasks aren't guaranteed to make your kid brilliant or secure them a full ride to college. I'm simply saying that everyone on earth has preferences and a certain way they function in the world. A lot of times I think we misunderstand what we're good at because we look at the task instead of the behavior.

So next time you watch your kid play, look closely at HOW they play. This can make frustrating situations like getting them to sit and eat at the dinner table a more pleasant experience if you know how they work. An old colleague of mine had a son that loved a good process. She would let him help pull out all of the ingredients for dinner and line them up, then walk through the recipe to create the meal. They would set the table the same way each evening, and once it was done they would load the dishwasher together. What kid would want to do that, right? Well, when you like a good process, you like to see one in action, and getting to participate makes it even better. Her son knew what to expect each time and that was comforting to him. He was a calmer and happier child at dinner, and mom got extra help too.

It will take time to get to know your kids, and as they grow they might shift, but when you are present with them and look past the task or activity, you might just find what they love.

YOUR BUSINESS IS AWESOME

Look around, what do you see? I see someone who has taken a big leap and created something they love. I see someone who works hard every day so that they can raise and nurture their business and set it free out in the world. I see someone who has love in their hearts and a fire in their eyes. I hope you see that too, because it's vital that you know how awesome you really are.

Who cares if other businesses make more money or got there faster than you? **SUCCESS IS JUST LIKE LOVE, IT HAS LIMITLESS CAPACITY. SOMEONE ELSE'S SUCCESS DOESN'T DIMINISH YOUR CHANCES OF BEING SUCCESSFUL. IN FACT, OTHER'S SUCCESSES PAVE THE WAY FOR YOURS.** They are like beacons in the night guiding you to where you want to go. Watch them, take notes, introduce yourself, and then take what you've learned and make it your own.

The next time you look at someone and what they have accomplished and begin to doubt yourself, stop. Stop and remember for a minute that you can create all of the opportunity you need to thrive. You may take a different path because we're all provided with unique circumstances, but there is always a way. The more you look longingly at others, the less you are looking inward to find the solution you need to lift you up to that same level of success. Or better yet, to surpass that person you revere so much. I recently heard the lovely business coach, Leah Remillet, say that when we compare ourselves to others we create an unnecessary ceiling for ourselves. We begin to see their goals as ours, and who's to say that our path has to stop where theirs did? Your destiny depends on what you decide, so set your path according to your goals, not someone else's.

29

Those Tough Days: A Method to Make Choosing Optimism Easier

Recently, I was waiting for a parking spot at the mall, and after the woman strapped her kid in the car seat she turned around and waved at me, giving me the signal that she saw I was waiting and would be moving shortly. It made my day!

I had an immediate flashback to my childhood, when my brother and I invented the 'Future Wavers of America' or FWA. We had decided the association would be for people who waved from their car when you let them in your lane, or waved to acknowledge they didn't mean to cut you off, or that they simply acknowledged that you were there, waiting for their spot, like that woman in the parking lot.

We thought that an FWA bumper sticker would be useful, because if you saw that someone had the sticker on their car, you would know they were a grateful, attentive person (and in the club). I don't know why we cared so much as kids about everyone having a mutual respect for each other, and caring enough to say thank you or I'm sorry when it was called for, but looking back, I think we were on to something.

As kids we saw the world with optimism. We recognized how little gestures can create a large impact in everyday lives. As adults we sometimes let that optimism get buried in the abyss of everyday life. You know that feeling you get when you get cut off on the way to work, people don't say thank you, or your kid gets pushed at school for no particular reason. We begin to wonder if the light in the world is starting to dim.

If only we could be more present in each other's lives, that would make all the difference in the world. That woman that waved at me that morning, she took the time to look up, see me, acknowledge me, and wave. That moment of being present only took her seconds, but it made my whole day. I'm taking a guess here, but I bet my smile and wave back had a positive effect on her too.

When we are present in each moment and try to look at the world without judgment, then we are able to accept and celebrate those around us. You might notice you say thank you more, because all of a sudden you see more for which to be thankful. You will become a magnet for smiles and conversation, because what you put out into the world you will attract back to you.

And it turns out, you don't even have to say a word to have a positive impact on someone's day; you just have to wave. Who knew it was that simple?

The key to making optimism easier in your life is to simply be present and grateful. If you want to get that happy feeling inside while making someone else feel good, I challenge you to simply wave. And just because you aren't in a car doesn't mean you can't join the challenge. Next time you see an opportunity to shake a hand, give a hug, a high-five, a chest bump, or a head nod (even virtual ones), do it. It will make you both smile, and it might just be the positive force that someone needs at that moment in their life.

30

The Importance of Letting Them Fall Down Every Once in a While

We hear a lot about how we should embrace our failures because they teach us, and help us move forward. We already know that's true, but what about the little trips and falls that aren't really failures, should we try to avoid those? That's a trick question. The answer is most definitely no.

Those scrapes and bruises your kids come home with each day, those are a visual proof that they lived that day without fear. They should be celebrated with cheers and love. **YOU DON'T GET SCRAPES UNLESS YOU DECIDED TO JUMP OR CLIMB, AND THAT'S THE ONLY WAY WE LEARN AND MOVE FORWARD.** Your child looked forward and charged ahead. Kids don't look down, they look forward. They see their destination and boldly go forth.

My son comes home pretty much every day with a new scrape and he doesn't seem to mind. I don't think he looks at them as a sign that he fell down, but more like normal wear and tear in order to get where he wants to go. As time passes he won't fall as much. He'll begin to run faster, and jump higher, because each day he is out there embracing the unknown.

There's a lesson to be learned from our children. We seek to teach them all we know, but we forget just how much our children have to teach us. When we go to the playground we see kids fall, dust themselves off, and then go right back to the playground. Sure, some of them cry and run to their mom, but who doesn't want a little love when we stumble?

Our children aren't even conscious of just how brave they really are. They stand and walk even though they've never done it before. They simply have this drive within them to develop and grow. They push forward, because forward is the only direction they know. It's truly an extraordinary thing to see.

I have what I call my pretend niece, who lost her leg from the knee down when she was one. She runs, swims, does gymnastics, and so much more. She doesn't recognize a challenge in her life. All she knows is that she wants to do everything anyone else can do, and she goes out and does it. Just like each of our children, she's an inspiration. Just as your love acts as a light that shines on your children, let them be a light that shines on you.

Each day in our home and in our business we make choices. We choose when to take risks, when to charge forward, and when to slow down, or stop. There will be a time when each of these actions are appropriate. What's important isn't that we always decided to charge forward. The important thing is to acknowledge when we're slowing down because it's the right thing to do in that situation, or because our fear is getting in our way. Take a deep breath and ask yourself why you decided to stop. If you find that you have a hard time being honest with yourself about why you aren't moving forward, then maybe it's time to reach out to your community, mastermind, or coach and see if you can get the support you need to push through.

We are meant to stumble and fall, that's why our skin is built to heal. So the next time you need a little inspiration to be brave, just look to your kids and remember just how brave they are each and every day, without even knowing it.

31

You're Doing Great, Mama!
How to Keep It All Going

How do you feel? Are you feeling the love? I hope so because I put a lot of love into writing this book, all with the intention of helping you see how amazing you really are. It's pretty much a love fest in here. Lots of room for love, and no room for guilt or judgment; those two weren't invited to the party.

You didn't know it was time to celebrate? Oh yeah, it sure is. Each of us has a journey and a calling, and you have chosen to listen to your passions in life and follow them. You are an inspiration to all of the other aspiring Boss Moms out there that might be looking for a little support these days. We all face different challenges in our lives, some more daunting than others, but that doesn't have to keep us down. It's our nature to rise up, get things done, pursue our dreams and show our kids how much we can accomplish when we have love, gratitude, compassion, and a little gumption in our lives.

REMEMBER THAT OUR ROLE AS PARENTS ISN'T TO GIVE UP OUR LIFE SO WE CAN RAISE OUR CHILDREN, IT'S TO SHOW THEM WHAT A GOOD LIFE LIVED LOOKS LIKE. It's our job to show them that 'work' doesn't have to be a negative word, to be the light that shines bright on our children and our business. You have so much to offer this world. Your family and business know this is true. Your friends, clients and community know it's true also. Make sure you believe it too, because you need to love yourself in order to love others. And if you have learned anything from this book, it's that love is the foundation to everything.

So put this book down, go give your kids a hug (or someone you love if you're not quite a mom yet) and go make it happen. The Boss Mom community will be here to support you along the way, and celebrate all of the amazing things you will do in your life, both big and small.

Thank you

Each time we do something new we learn. Writing Boss Mom has been one of the most fascinating learning experiences of my life. I learned what it takes to write a book, and wow does it a take a lot of effort, but also yields a lot of reward. I hope you choose to write a book at some point in your life. I know each of us has a story to tell, and I believe that the writing process can really help you find your purpose; that's exactly what it did for me.

I also discovered something amazing, that we are not alone. I never realized just how many of us Boss Moms are out there simply trying to be a mom, entrepreneur, and woman all at the same time. In writing this book I found a community I didn't even realize existed, and it has been such a powerful force in my life. Thank you for being part of that community, and for trusting in me. I know that all of us Boss Moms don't have a ton of time to spare, and I am truly honored that you chose to spend some of your precious time with me.

If you enjoyed Boss Mom, then I would be eternally grateful if you left a review. Simply go to www.boss-mom.com/bookreview, which will redirect you to the Boss Mom Amazon page. Scroll down until you see the Customer Reviews and click 'Write a Customer Review'. Reviews help other Boss Moms know if the book has been useful to other women. I would love to touch as many lives as I can with the book and start the official Boss Mom Movement. Thank you, you rock!

Don't forget that you can download all of the exercises in the book at **www.boss-mom.com/BMBresources**. I want to help make it as easy as possible to help you move forward and make your Boss Mom world a little easier, and I think these downloads can help.

If you're looking for a good, supportive, community, then make sure to join our Boss Moms Facebook Group at **www.boss-moms.com/join**. I can't wait to see you there.

And if you want to connect with me then you can find me on Instagram, Twitter, and Periscope at @DanaMalstaff, I love to meet new members to the community so stop by and say hello.

If you would like to have Dana speak at an event please visit **www.boss-mom.com/speak**

Made in the USA
Lexington, KY
12 December 2017